PRACTICAL
DECOUPAGE

PRACTICAL DECOUPAGE

DENISE THOMAS AND MARY FOX

PHOTOGRAPHY BY
DEBBIE PATTERSON

Trafalgar Square Publishing
NORTH POMFRET, VERMONT

First published in the United States of America in 1993 by
Trafalgar Square Publishing, North Pomfret, Vermont 05053

First published in Great Britain in 1993
by Anaya Publishers Ltd, Strode House,
44-50 Osnaburgh Street, London NW1 3ND

Managing Editor *Jane Struthers*
Designer *Carol McCleeve*
Photographer *Debbie Patterson*
Styling Assistant *Camilla Bambrough*
Illustrator *Coral Mula*
Reference Photography *Alastair Thorpe*
Historical Photography *Tom Ramm*

ISBN 0-943955-78-5

Library of Congress Catalog Card Number: 93-60186

Typeset in Great Britain by
Bookworm Typesetting, Manchester
Colour reproduction by Scantrans Pte Ltd, Singapore
Printed and bound in Hong Kong by Dah Hua Printing Co Ltd

— Contents —

INTRODUCTION

*I*n this book we hope to teach you, step-by-step, the art of découpage. It is not difficult, but it is a craft and it can often be an art form too. The basic process involves cutting out paper images and glueing them on to objects, but that is only part of the technique, because it is up to the craftsman or woman to create a pleasing decoration which complements the object to which it is being applied.

Part of the great pleasure of découpage is searching for the articles you are going to work on, which can involve anything from visiting jumble sales, boot fairs and junk (thrift) shops to ships' chandlers and anywhere else that will yield good pickings. We have both spent many happy hours travelling to these places and looking for suitable objects. You will soon learn to keep your eyes open, and that will also apply to looking for prints, pictures or wrapping paper with which to decorate the objects. You'll become attuned to spotting suitable

Floral images are ideal for découpage.

découpage articles in a very short time. If you always buy your objects for découpage from a particular shop, the owner will probably soon get a good idea of the sort of things you are looking for and may even keep suitable items to one side for you. Friends and family

who are having tidy-ups or clear-outs from time to time may also unearth suitable objects that they think are fit only for throwing out but which are just the sort of thing you are looking for.

Everyone has a different approach to découpage and will use different prints and papers, and that's one of the many reasons it is such an interesting and, indeed, therapeutic, pastime. We both have découpage techniques that vary slightly, as you will see in this book, but they are simply two different aspects of the same craft. Denise specializes in ageing antique and old pieces, which calls for a very different technique from Mary's work, which involves applying a highly lacquered finish to her objects. You will find many examples of these techniques in this book, and together we will show you how to découpage a tremendous variety of objects, from simple table mats to candlesticks and toy boxes, with plenty of other ideas along the way. A great deal of patience is required if your découpaging is to be successful, for it isn't a craft that can be hurried, but the results of your hard work will be well worth while and a source of satisfaction.

Happy découpaging!
DENISE THOMAS AND MARY FOX

Without the support and love of both my parents and my four sons, Christopher, Andrew, Nicolas and Sean, I could not have achieved what I have and so I wish to dedicate my part of this book to my 'four sons' who, fortunately or unfortunately, have followed their old mother in the arts and all work in a creative capacity.

Denise Thomas

As always, great thanks are to Fiona, Duncan and Nicholas for always being there and encouraging their dotty mother with their love and support, and also to June Woodford and Mary Friend for their patience and self-control in teaching me découpage.

Mary Fox

THE HISTORY OF DECOUPAGE

Découpage is an old craft which was first heard of in the twelfth and thirteenth centuries. It was reputed to have been a European folk art but reached a much wider audience in seventeenth-century Venice, when it was used to embellish painted furniture.

At the time, there was a great demand for the heavily lacquered furniture being produced in China and Japan, but it was so expensive that few people could afford to buy it. Undaunted, the Venetian craftsmen decided to use découpage to imitate the lacquered furniture, and it became a great success. The guilds created their own designs and coloured them, then cut them out and pasted them on to the furniture in just the same way as we will show you in this book. The craftsmen then lacquered the furniture repeatedly until the images appeared to sink into the wood and looked as though they had been hand-painted. The technique was known as *arte povero* or *lacche povero* which means, literally, 'the poor man's lacquer'.

This Venetian craft was so successful that it had spread to France by the eighteenth century, with the most famous French découpage craftsman being Jean Baptiste Fillement, who was particularly noted for his Chinese lacquer techniques. It was the French who coined the word *découpage* from their verb *découper*, which means 'to cut'. Among the many famous people who practised the art was the ill-fated Marie Antoinette, plus all the members of her court. Beau Brummel, the famous dandy who had been a leader of society in England and a great friend of the Prince Regent (later King George IV), also became enthralled by découpage after he moved to France to escape his huge gambling debts. Some beautiful items of furniture were produced, but sadly very valuable pictures were often cut up in the process because, unlike the Venetians who had always painted their own pictures specially for the craft, the French preferred to use existing pictures no matter how much they were worth or who had painted them.

Découpage was taken to Britain during the Victorian age, probably by people returning from the Grand Tour of Europe which was so popular in those days. Prints of all descriptions were cut up and used to adorn sewing boxes, screens and many other household articles. The Victorians had a passion for decorating and, with the advent of cheap colour printing processes, began to publish books

of scraps – illustrations that were specially produced to be cut out and used as decorations. Sailors voyaging overseas would collect souvenirs, such as boxes, sea chests and other mementoes, which they would bring home with them and were often decorated with découpage by their families.

One of the most famous modern exponents of découpage is the American, Hiram Manning, who also taught the craft. Examples of his work, and that of his pupils, is on show in various museums around the world and they are truly inspiring. Two other renowned découpage artists were both women. Mary Delaney was famous for her exquisite cutting and pasting of flower miniatures, many of which are exhibited at the Victoria and Albert Museum in London. Looking at her work today it is hard to imagine how she was able to make her découpage so fine and delicate. Caroline Duer was famous in America in the 1940s for her work, although she followed the Biedermeier style of decoration which had been created in Germany in the 1820s. Today, découpage is enjoying a great revival of interest all over the world, and we hope this brief summary of its history, plus the rest of our book, will lead you to discover more about this fascinating and exciting craft so you can create your own découpage antiques for the future.

Many museums for the decorative arts display examples of découpage work from the past. The photographs on these two pages show four different types of antique découpage work. **FACING PAGE** *This is a Venetian casket which was made between 1725-50.* **THIS PAGE, RIGHT** *This stoneware vase has been decorated with découpage.* **FAR RIGHT** *This vase has been decorated in an oriental style.* **TOP** *The Victorians thoroughly enjoyed découpage and albums of suitable scraps were published especially for the craft.*

STEP-BY-STEP
——— GUIDE ———

Some of the objects suitable for découpage.

On the following pages we will take you through the basic découpage processes step by step, and show you how to make seven different projects. For each one, we explain the découpage techniques, plus any other information you need to know, and then go over the basic points again with step-by-step photographs, so you can see exactly what you have to do.

Even so, don't feel daunted by the prospect of learning découpage because it is very easy and all you really need is plenty of time and patience. Even if you don't feel very confident about your design skills at this stage you will soon learn to develop your 'eye' and will, as everyone does, learn from your mistakes. The projects in this section range from the very simple, such as the table mats, to slightly more complicated ones, such as a bedroom chair. Even so, they are all easy to make and, we hope, you will enjoy learning these basic découpage steps.

DENISE THOMAS

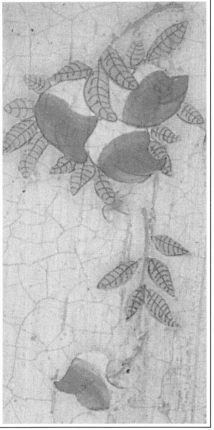

It is always important to choose images that will complement the style and shape of the objects you wish to decorate, but it is especially so when working on small pieces like this finger plate, door knob and keyhole cover. You must choose images that are suitably delicate without being so small that they get lost in the final decoration or look bitty or fussy.

Door Furniture

It is easy to decorate door furniture like this, and these pieces are an excellent example of how découpage can transform very ordinary household objects into works of art in their own right.

As you look through the photographs in this book you will see that we use two different techniques when découpaging objects – we either give them an extremely shiny, lacquered, finish or we give them an antiqued finish, with plenty of cracks

and a darker coloured antique glaze. Each of the finishes serves a different purpose and is chosen to complement the object that has been decorated. Usually, objects which are given the antique finish are already old, but in this case I decided to age some modern plastic items.

After choosing a suitable paper with plenty of small but strong birds and flowers on it, it was time to choose a base colour for the paint, and I opted for a very pale green. While the second coat of paint was drying I cut out the images with a scalpel knife. This was very fiddly because I didn't want to make mistakes.

I arranged the cut-outs on the different pieces of door furniture until I was happy with the way they looked, then glued them in place and, when the glue had dried, applied a coat of craqueleur to produce an aged appearance, followed by an antique glaze which I rubbed in to emphasize the cracks of the craqueleur, and then began to build up the many coats of varnish until the cut-outs had completely sunk into the varnish and looked as though they had been painted on by hand.

STEP-BY-STEP GUIDE

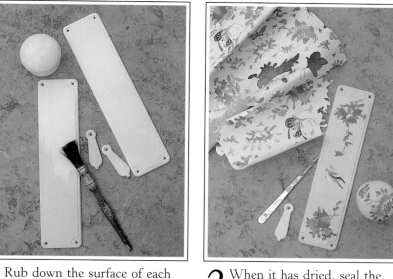

1 Rub down the surface of each piece with fine wire (steel) wool or sandpaper to give a good key for the paint. Apply two coats of emulsion (latex) paint to each piece.

2 When it has dried, seal the paint with a thin coat of varnish. Cut out the images and decide where to place them on the objects. Apply glue to the objects and the undersides of the cut-outs. Place the cut-outs in position, press down with a clean cloth and leave to dry.

3 Apply the first coat of varnish to each object and leave it until it is just dry to the touch, then apply the craqueleur. Encourage the cracks to form with a hair-drier. Leave to dry thoroughly.

4 Rub antique glaze into the cracks and wipe off the surplus. Leave to dry then begin to apply the varnish, building up at least 15 coats for durability. Polish with beeswax.

Fire Bucket

This fire bucket is one of several that I found at a boot sale, so I was able to experiment with different decorative finishes – a bucket with a tartan background is shown on pages 66-7.

When you find an old bucket like this you must look beyond its grime, flaking paint and generally tatty appearance to what can be done with it once you've got it home. Rust can be removed with a proprietary rust remover, holes can be filled with special fillers and, with a little imagination, you can transform something that was in a dreadfully battered state into an object of beauty.

To remove the rust on this bucket, I rubbed off all the flaking paint with a wire brush and then roughly sanded the surface with a sheet of coarse sandpaper. To check for holes, which are sometimes too small to be seen with the naked eye, I immersed the bucket in water – any air bubbles that appear on the bucket will indicate a hole, which you can repair with car filler. After sanding down the filler I applied a coat of rust remover and waited for it to dry before washing it all off with white spirit (paint thinner). The next step was to paint on two coats of an anti-rust/primer. After the second coat had dried thoroughly I was ready to start decorating the bucket.

STEP-BY-STEP GUIDE

DENISE THOMAS

When working on an old bucket like this it is very important to prepare it properly for decoration and not take short cuts when sanding it down or removing the rust. You may think you save time by only brushing off the rust and not treating it with a rust remover, but you will realize your folly when the rust comes through later on and ruins your finished piece of work, so be warned!

1 It doesn't matter how battered or tatty your bucket looks because you will be stripping it right back to the metal. Start by rubbing away all the loose paint with a wire brush and sandpaper.

2 Examine the bucket and handle for rust holes, repair with car filler and leave to dry. Roughly smooth down with sandpaper. Rub all the rust away then paint on rust remover and leave to dry.

3 Prime the surface of the bucket with a coat of anti-rust paint made specially for metal objects and leave to dry. Apply at least two coats of emulsion (latex) in the base colour, choosing a different colour for the inside, and seal with thin varnish.

4 Cut out the images with a scalpel or cuticle scissors and glue on to the bucket. Press down firmly and allow to dry. Apply a coat of matt (flat) varnish and leave to dry. Apply the craqueleur and leave to dry. Rub on the antique glaze, wipe off the excess and leave to dry. Rub gold paste around the rim, rubbing some off again, and leave to dry. Apply up to 20 coats of varnish and finish with a wax polish.

——— TABLE MATS ———

Table mats are easy projects to work on when you have just begun découpage because they are inexpensive to buy, have flat surfaces and are quick to make. These table mats were made for me specially from MDF (medium-density fibreboard), but you could use existing table mats if you prefer, having first cleaned off any decorations.

MDF has a very smooth surface so doesn't need any preliminary treatment, but it must be sanded down to provide a key for the paint. If you are using old mats you will have to sand them down too. Now you are ready to apply a coat of undercoat and leave it to dry. If your mats are made from MDF they will go slightly fluffy at this stage, so sand them down again until they are perfectly smooth before painting on your base colour. You can use emulsion (latex) or oil-based paint for this, and need to apply two or three coats.

After glueing on the cut-outs and waiting for them to dry, I started to apply my coats of matt (flat) varnish. After about fifteen coats I sanded the mats down with medium to fine wet and dry paper, rubbing in a circular motion. This leaves a white

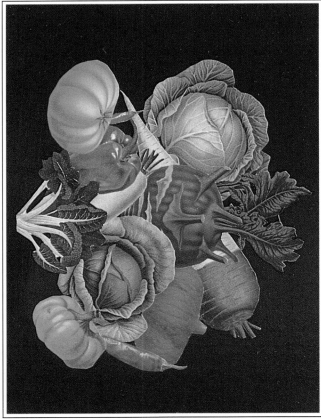

MARY FOX

16

scum which you should wipe off with a clean soft cloth. I applied two coats of satin varnish, and, when the second coat had dried, sanded down again with very fine wet and dry paper. After wiping off the scum and dust I applied a final coat of varnish. After it had dried, I made up a paste of rottenstone powder and baby oil and firmly rubbed it into each mat. This creates a tough and heat-resistant finish which can be washed with warm water and a soft cloth. Finally, I glued on the felt backing.

I used images of all sorts of vegetables to decorate these mats, but you could choose designs to match the colour scheme of your dining room or a favourite set of china.

STEP-BY-STEP GUIDE

1 Apply one coat of undercoat to the face of each table mat – in this case, gesso for a smooth surface. Leave to dry then apply two or three coats of base paint.

2 Cut out the motifs and protect each one with a coat of sealer. Arrange the motifs on the mats until you are happy with the way they look, then glue in position.

3 Press down hard on each motif, then leave to dry for 24 hours. Begin to apply the coats of matt (flat) varnish. After about 15 coats, sand down with wet and dry paper.

4 Apply two coats of satin varnish, sand down, apply a final coat of varnish and leave to dry. Rub in rottenstone powder. Place mat on felt, cut around it and glue on the felt.

DENISE THOMAS

KITCHEN PANELS

Découpage isn't just suitable for decorative objects – you can also apply the technique to pieces of furniture and, in this case, my own kitchen. To begin painting a cupboard, rub it down with sandpaper, apply a coat of wood sealer and leave to dry, then paint on a coat of wood primer and leave to dry again. You are now ready to apply your base coat of emulsion (latex) paint. In the past, paint was made from lead and one of the undercoats that was frequently used was red lead, so I made up a red undercoat to give an authentic and aged effect. I blended a red emulsion paint with terracotta (red oxide) powdered paint, using an old egg beater as the paint has to be mixed thoroughly. Add a little water until the paint is the consistency of thick cream. Now brush it on to the doors heavily and thickly. Leave to dry and apply at least one or two more coats.

When my final coat of red paint was dry, I mixed up some green emulsion paint with green powder paint – I tinted mine with acrylic paint until I got the depth of colour that I needed. Apply two coats of this new colour, leaving the first one

to dry before applying the second. When that one is dry, take some wire (steel) wool and rub the paint where the green top coat would have been worn away with general wear and tear (for instance, around the handles, the edges of the cupboards and at the corners). Don't be frightened of rubbing off

These are the panels that I have decorated in my kitchen and they have received many compliments and admiring glances. They conceal my washing machine, refrigerator and freezer, so in a way are doubly decorative.

18

STEP-BY-STEP GUIDE

1 Rub down any existing paint or polish, then paint each door or panel with a coat of wood primer. Leave to dry then apply two coats of red undercoat.

2 Rub down with wire (steel) wool. Paint on the base colour – emulsion (latex) mixed with powder pigment. Rub down again with wire wool, so some red shows through.

3 Seal the cut-outs before arranging them on the doors or panels to see which is the best position for them. All doors can match or each one can be different.

4 Glue the cut-outs in place and press down. Allow to dry. Apply the first coat of varnish then the craqueleur, antique glaze and at least 20 coats of varnish.

the paint – you can even have patches where you have rubbed away to the original wood. By the way, I would strongly recommend that you wear a face mask for this job because the paint dust will fly everywhere and can be toxic. If you have sensitive eyes you might like to wear a pair of goggles.

Brush the dust off each panel, apply one coat of sealer and leave to dry. You are now ready to glue on your cut-out decorations, which you should do in the normal way. Complete the antiquing découpage treatment (see pages 102-5), ending with a final coat of a good antique wax.

—— CACHE POTS ——

These cache pots are a good example of how easy and effective it is to transform modern objects into attractive examples of découpage. They are good projects to experiment with when you are just beginning to discover découpage because they are relatively inexpensive to buy, don't need much preparation and are quick to decorate.

Because these pots were going to be used as plant holders, I wanted to decorate them with suitably floral images and made each one different – one was decorated with cut-outs of a pink clematis and the other with cut-outs of white hellebores and scarlet poinsettias. The colours of the flowers were so vivid that I decided to paint the pots black, so they would look as dramatic as possible.

Cutting out the clematis flowers and leaves was quite fiddly because of all the tendrils and buds, and so was not a job to be hurried – it is very annoying to realize you have just sliced through a flower or leaf because your concentration lapsed for a few seconds. Of course, you do not have to decorate the cache pots with flowers and could choose interesting pictures of leaves instead, or even berries or fruits. Sometimes it is worthwhile thinking about which plant you will put in the cache pot when it has been decorated, and then choose some cut-outs that will complement that plant.

An important point to remember when glueing on large cut-outs like the ones shown here is to ensure there are no air bubbles or lumps of glue trapped between the pot and the cut-outs – the larger the cut-out the more likely this is to happen. Don't worry unduly if the cut-out is slightly larger than the pot, because you can cut off any excess paper at the base – if you look at the large photograph showing the two finished pots, you will see that I trimmed one of the hellebore leaves so it was flush with the bottom of the pot.

These cache pots are quick and easy to decorate if you are new to découpage. They are also very useful household objects and make marvellous presents for plant-loving friends. You may wish to consider the decorative scheme of your room when choosing suitable cut-outs for these cache pots, or find images that complement the plants they will contain.

MARY FOX

STEP-BY-STEP GUIDE

1 These pots are plastic so must be sanded down first to give a good key for the paint. Apply one coat of undercoat, then two to three coats of the base colour – in this case, black emulsion (latex).

2 Cut out the motifs and choose their positions. Apply glue to the undersides of the cut-outs and the surface of the pot, moisten your fingers with a little water and rub the glue on the pot.

3 Place the cut-outs on the glued surface of the pot, pressing each one down firmly with a small rubber roller or a soft clean cloth to push out all surplus glue and any air bubbles. Clean off excess glue and leave to dry.

4 Apply 12 to 15 coats of varnish, then sand down with medium to fine wet and dry paper. Apply two coats of satin varnish, sand down again with very fine sandpaper and apply two final coats of satin varnish.

MARY FOX

When I found this chair it was nestling in a jumble of an antique shop and badly needed attention. I treated it for woodworm and, because they were so large, even had to fill some of the holes left by the insects. We do not usually recommend filling these holes because they add to the antiquity and personality of the finished piece, but sometimes it is necessary.

Victorian Chair

When I bought this chair, woodworm had munched its way through much of it, leaving large holes. Although the previous owner of the chair assured me that the woodworm was inactive, I treated all the holes with a proprietary woodworm killer just to be on the safe side. Some of the worm holes were so large they needed filling with wood filler, but not enough to ruin the antiquity and character of the chair. When the filler had dried, I applied a coat of gesso to give a smooth surface.

I had been commissioned to decorate the chair to match someone's bedroom, so painted it in a blue base coat, adding blue artists' oil paint to an oil-based paint until I had the colour I wanted. I glued on the cut-outs, then began the lengthy task of applying my twenty coats of matt (flat) varnish. After the final coat I sanded the chair hard, then applied a single coat of satin varnish, sanded again and applied a second coat of satin varnish. Before you do this, do make sure you have wiped off all the varnish dust from the surface, otherwise you will just varnish it in place and have to sand it all down again when the varnish has dried. Finally, I gave the chair a padded seat – I cut out the required shape from a pillow, covered it with a plain cotton fabric and then with a pale blue silk that matched both the paint colour and the cut-outs. You can add a toning braid if you wish.

STEP-BY-STEP GUIDE

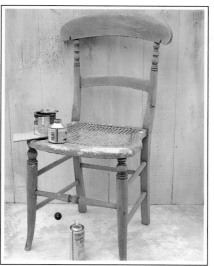

1 If the seat is damaged it must be removed and replaced. Clean the woodwork with a clean cloth dipped in white spirit (paint thinner).

2 Check for woodworm and treat every hole. Fill in very large holes with wood filler and sand down. Apply one coat of gesso as an undercoat.

3 Make up a suitable base colour using a pale blue oil-based paint mixed with artists' oils. Apply two to three coats, letting each one dry before applying the next one. Cut out the images you will be using for the chair.

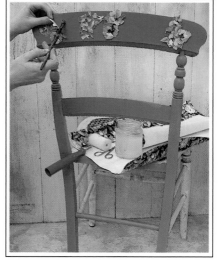

4 Apply the cut-outs. Mix dark blue oil paint with varnish and use to highlight some of the round pieces on the chair. Leave to dry thoroughly, then apply about 15 coats of varnish. Sand down with wet and dry sandpaper.

5 Apply two coats of satin varnish, sand down again and then apply the final coat of varnish. Mix rottenstone powder with baby oil and buff well, or use polish. Cut an old pillow to fit the seat and cover with fabric. Cut out the cover and fit to the seat.

TERRACOTTA POT

Terracotta pots like the one shown here are marvellous for découpage work, yet they are seldom used for that purpose. As a result they are very interesting because they are different from the usual articles decorated with découpage. It also shows that virtually anything can be découpaged!

This pot didn't need any cleaning, but it did have to be painted with a sealer before I could decorate it – terracotta is very absorbent and the paint would have disappeared into the clay if it had been applied direct. When the sealer had dried I painted the pot in its base colour, which was parchment-coloured, using rough criss-cross brush strokes to give a textured finish. The interior of the pot was painted with a blue emulsion (latex) mixed with blue acrylic paints until it matched the colours of

the cut-outs. I chose this decorative effect because the cut-outs were pictures of needlepoint flowers on a fabric background, so the canvas-like appearance of the paint matched it well.

After the paint had dried thoroughly I mixed up an antique glaze, made from a mixture of glaze, white spirit (paint thinner), raw umber artists' oil paint and black oil paint, and rubbed it gently all over the pot with a soft clean cloth. After it had been allowed to dry for twenty-four hours, the cut-outs were applied, and I followed the other découpage processes of varnishing and polishing in the usual way (see pages 100-2). As the finish on terracotta doesn't have to be of such good quality as fine woodwork, I only sanded the varnish once before applying the final two coats of varnish.

STEP-BY-STEP GUIDE

It is strange how difficult it can be sometimes to choose the right design for découpage. In this case, although the pot was reminiscent of Greek urns it had a modern shape that meant the Greek images, which I had originally chosen, looked completely wrong. Although the pot was going to contain plants, flower cut-outs didn't look right either. Finally, I decided these needlepoint flowers looked best.

MARY FOX

1 This pot was bought new, so did not have to be cleaned. However, terracotta is porous and would have absorbed all the paint so the pot had to be sealed. Spray on a fine mist of sealer.

2 Choose the cut-outs, then paint the pot in suitable colours. Paint the outside of the pot with parchment-coloured emulsion (latex) paint. Paint the inside of the pot with a blue emulsion paint.

3 Leave the paint to dry thoroughly, then apply an antique glaze over the outside of the pot. Make up the glaze with glaze, white spirit (paint thinner), raw umber artists' oil paint and black oil paints. Rub this mixture all over the pot with a soft clean cloth and leave to dry.

4 Glue on the cut-outs, making sure there are no air bubbles and that all the edges are stuck down. Leave to dry, then begin to apply the many coats of varnish. Sand down the 18th coat, then apply two more coats of varnish.

FINISHED PROJECTS

Some of the finished projects in this section.

In this section, we will show you a small selection of some of the découpage projects we have made in the course of our interest in the craft. For each one, we explain what we did and why we did it, and also give hints on solving problems that may arise when you work on similar projects yourself. Each project is accompanied by photographs, and often detail photographs too, so you can see them clearly.

As in the previous section of this book, the projects we have chosen vary considerably in scope, expertise and time. Some of them are very simple and are ideal if you are a newcomer to this fascinating craft, while others, such as the large trunks, the glass bowl and the jewellery box, are probably best attempted when you are more confident about your work.

——— Victorian Hip Bath ———

*T*he moment I saw this hip bath, I was determined to buy it and give it the decorative treatment it deserved. Part of its attraction was definitely the wonderfully curved and generous shape, and I especially liked the two arm rests on either side of the bath.

Luckily, the crackled paint on the outside of the bath was so attractive and in a good enough condition that I was able to leave it in its original state, so I matched its colour on the rest of the bath. It was important to maintain that antique effect throughout, so after rubbing down the old paint on the inside of the bath in the usual way and treating it with an all-purpose metal primer, I applied a couple of base coats of lemon-coloured emulsion (latex) paint using rough cross-hatched strokes. I then applied an antique glaze to give an aged effect. I also painted a dark outline around the edge of the bath. I chose large rich-looking flowers and fruits for the decoration and glued them on in the usual way, then applied the first coat of varnish followed by a coat of craqueleur.

An antique glaze completes the aged appearance by accentuating the cracks, so I dipped a clean cloth into the glaze and put a small dab of raw umber oil paint on it, then rubbed it in a circular motion all over the hip bath. I then rubbed off the excess glaze, taking care to leave it in the cracks. After leaving it to dry for several days, I started to apply the coats of matt (flat) varnish, and finished it with antique polish.

I wanted to make this hip bath look as though it had been randomly coloured by age and use, so put less antique glaze on the areas that would have had the most wear (in this case, the back and base) and applied more to the sides.

DENISE THOMAS

——— Decorated Glass Bowl ———

As we have both said and shown throughout this book, a huge variety of articles and surfaces can be découpaged and most of them involve very straight-forward techniques. Glass, however, is a completely different matter, because of its see-through qualities. Even so, you shouldn't be deterred from trying, although it is advisable to experiment on some cheap and ordinary objects before beginning work on anything that is expensive to replace or very complicated.

This bowl was no doubt once the home of a lonely and rather cramped goldfish. The first step was to wash the bowl thoroughly, inside and out, with warm soapy water until it was so clean it sparkled. I then rinsed it well and left it to dry upside down. I wanted to decorate the bowl in a circular design which would mimic the movement of water, so chose a suitable paper. After cutting it out, I arranged it on the outside of the bowl to get an idea of how it would look and, when satisfied with the effect, started the glueing process.

I made the glue rather more runny than usual, then painted it over one half of the glass on the inside of the bowl and rubbed it into a very smooth paste with my fingers, which I had first dipped in clean water. Then, I started positioning the cut-outs inside the bowl, but with the images facing outwards (otherwise all you would see on the outside of the bowl would be the back of each cut-out), rubbing each one with my knuckles to ensure it was firm before going on to the next one. When I had completed one half of the inside of the bowl in this way I repeated the process with the other half, then left the bowl for 24 hours. When I was sure that all the cut-outs were thoroughly glued on I painted a fixative over them.

I was now ready to start painting the bowl with emulsion (latex) paint. It wasn't too difficult to paint the lower section of the bowl because I just turned it round with one hand while holding the paintbrush, loaded with paint, in the other. However, that became impossible near the lip of the bowl so I used a small piece of soft foam rubber soaked in paint instead, and continued to turn the bowl in the same way as before. After the first coat had dried I applied another one, followed by several coats of varnish inside and out.

This bowl was decorated to contain flowers, but if I had intended it to become a lamp I would have

MARY FOX

It can take quite a lot of practice to decorate a piece of glass successfully, so it is a good idea to experiment first with something inexpensive and easy before going on to more complicated shapes. One of the most important points to remember is that the right sides of the cut-outs will be glued to the inside of the bowl, so they can be seen through the glass. This can be a very fiddly and time-consuming process, so be patient!

used an opaline paint as a base coat, glued circles of aluminium foil, about 3cm/1¼in in diameter, over the paint and then varnished over the surface so the light from the bulb inside the bowl would have shone through them. A hole for the cord would also have been drilled through the base. Alternatively, you could turn the bowl into a very attractive and unusual lamp base by drilling a hole through the base, making a circular stopper for the mouth of the bowl with a large piece of cork and placing a bulb holder in the centre, with an ordinary shade held over the top.

On no account be tempted to place lighted candles inside the glass bowl so the light shines through them, because the varnish is highly inflammable and could easily catch alight.

DENISE THOMAS

MILITARY TRAY

*W*hen I was approached to paint and decorate this tray I had to think hard how to go about it. It was to be a presentation piece which would be displayed in the mess hall of the Royal Military School of Music in Twickenham, Middlesex, near London, England, so I wanted to link the two themes of music and the military in some way.

I was very lucky to be given photocopies of the figures of the military bandsmen and also the central illustration of the Royal Military School of Music itself. They were all black and white, and I thought they would show up best against a deep red base colour. The tray itself was new, so didn't need any restoration work. Instead, I gave it an all-over coat of wood primer which I allowed to dry thoroughly before painting on three coats of bright red emulsion (latex). Even though the tray was new I wanted to make it look as old as possible, so painted on the emulsion with criss-cross brush strokes to give an antique cross-hatched effect.

After that, it was a simple matter to arrange the cut-outs on the tray, placing the picture of the building in the centre and grouping the military bandsmen around it. After glueing them on and making absolutely sure there were no air bubbles or lumps of glue trapped underneath any of the cut-outs, but especially the central one because of its size, I carefully wrote the name of its regiment by each figure, using a gold pen. After the paint had dried thoroughly I followed all my usual antiquing processes of applying craqueleur and antique glaze. If you look at the photograph showing the tray in detail you will see how I have rubbed antique glaze into the paintwork in the middle of the tray, to simulate the dirt that would have gathered there over years of use.

Finally, after building up about twenty coats of varnish and rubbing in a good antique polish, I glued a piece of green felt to the underside of the tray, in case it was going to sit on an antique piece of furniture.

I thoroughly enjoyed making this tray and, although this one was specially commissioned and has a military theme, you can easily adapt the idea to suit your own design. The trickiest part is glueing the large central cut-out in place, because it is all too easy to have air bubbles or small lumps of glue trapped underneath the image.

33

COFFEE POTS

*Y*ou can find enamel coffee pots like the ones shown here in junk shops, boot fairs and other découpage hunting grounds, but do try to find old ones because many of them are new and aren't quite the same.

When I bought these pots they weren't rusty but I still painted each one with a good-quality anti-rust paint that is also a primer. I applied two light coats to each pot, just to be on the safe side, then painted on the base colour, having chosen a greeny-black that would complement the cut-outs I'd found. I painted each coat with cross-hatching strokes to give the pots a nice old look, but chose a lighter colour for the interior of each pot. This is simple until you come to the spout, when it can take patience and a long brush to ensure you have painted as much of the spout's interior as you possibly can. Look carefully and critically down the spout from all angles to ensure you haven't missed any patches, because it is extremely annoying suddenly to spot a gap when you thought you had finished work on the piece.

When I was pleased with the effect I left the pots to dry thoroughly, then started to play around with the cut-outs, deciding exactly where to put them on each pot. The smaller pot on the left was given a very muted design, while the larger pot on the right was given a brighter design of cherries.

To enhance the aged appearance of the pots I painted them with craqueleur, then applied my usual antique glaze and at least twenty coats of varnish. Finally, I gave the pots a good polish with beeswax to bring up a lovely sheen.

You won't be able to serve coffee, or anything else, in the pots when you have découpaged them because the varnish would taint the liquid, but they are very attractive decorations. As with all découpaged articles, you should keep the pots out of strong sunlight and try to avoid knocking them as you could chip the paint.

Be careful not to overdo the decorations when working on relatively small items like these pots, or you will spoil their finished appearance.

DENISE THOMAS

——— PAIR OF ARMY DIXIES ———

*W*hen I discovered these two dixies they were very rusty and it was only when I started to clean off all the rust that I found the bases were solid copper. That was a real bonus, but I must admit that an awful lot of elbow grease, sweat and tears went into cleaning the copper to bring it back to its original state, although it was well worth it in the end.

When they were used for their original purpose, these dixies would have been used in army canteens or carried into the field. Unfortunately the canisters that would have once sat inside, for such things as hot soup or army tea, had long since disappeared, but even so I could see that, when painted and decorated, these dixies would be able to take pride of place in someone's kitchen.

I decided to forget any army theme for the dixies and opted instead for a variety of leaves and fruits, such as pears and apples, that would complement almost any kitchen or dining area. Because the dixies match I could have given them identical decorations, but I thought they would look much nicer if they were different. If you are lucky enough to find anything like these dixies I would not recommend putting hot tea or coffee in them, firstly because it might spoil your decorations and secondly, the varnish and finishing coat of polish will taint the liquid.

These dixies can never be used again to contain liquids, but they would be very useful containers for dried foods or could just be decorative objects in their own right.

DENISE THOMAS

36

TEA URN

*O*nce you start to look around boot fairs, junk shops and other fascinating places you will be astonished at the diversity of objects that are on sale, and probably be quickly filled with ideas for ways of decorating them. When I saw this tea urn, looking very sad and forlorn, I had to buy it because I could instantly see its possibilities.

During their working life tea urns normally look very drab and boring, so I thought it would be fun to decorate this urn in a rich way that would accentuate its rounded shape and the lovely old wooden handle and brass tap (spigot). I decided to use a design of rosy red apples against a deep green background.

When I got the tea urn home, my first job was to clean up the wooden handle, which was completely covered with thick treacle-like paint. To do this, I removed the gungy paint with paint stripper. Always wear a pair of good-quality rubber gloves when doing this, as the acid in the paint stripper can cause nasty burns if it comes into contact with your skin – if that happens, rinse the affected part under the cold tap immediately. It is also a good idea to use paint stripper out of doors if possible, but certainly in a well-ventilated room to avoid breathing in the fumes. I then polished the handle with antique polish and cleaned the brass tap with fine wire (steel) wool and a chrome cleaner made for cars, finishing with a brass polish. After that, I prepared and decorated the tea urn in the usual way, and painted its interior with a plain contrast colour.

Prowling around boot fairs and nosing through antique shops and around jumble sales is half the fun of découpage because you never know what you are going to find. You will swiftly learn to look beyond the dirt and grime to the object's true potential, as I did here with this tea urn.

DENISE THOMAS

——— Green Casserole Dish ———

*T*his is a casserole dish that could no longer be used for cooking but was ideal for découpage. Because the handles divided the base of the dish into two halves, I decided to decorate each half with slightly different images.

Having sanded down the enamel surface I painted the outside of the casserole dish and lid with dark green emulsion (latex) paint, which would provide an effective contrast with the golden yellow of the bird and leaf designs. The inside of the casserole dish was roughly painted in a paler green colour.

It took some time to place the cut-outs of the birds and leaves in exactly the right position, as I wanted them to butt up to the rim of the dish. I decided to have a different decorative effect for the lid and chose cut-outs of butterflies and flowers. To give a thoroughly aged appearance, I followed my usual antiquing technique – the cracks produced by the craqueleur showed up particularly well against the golden tones of the birds and leaves and I was very happy with the finished casserole dish. It makes an excellent storage container for dry foods or other kitchen items.

DENISE THOMAS

This casserole dish is yet another good example of the way découpage can give a new lease of life to what was originally a sad-looking object fit only for the scrap heap. You will find many other items that we have rescued in this book.

40

—— DEEP BLUE EDWARDIAN JUG ——

*T*his enamel jug was probably originally the ewer *that stood on someone's wash stand, along with a large washing bowl. However, when I found it at a local jumble sale it had long since lost its companion and was sitting sadly by itself.*

Enamel jugs like this one are often rather chipped and battered when you find them, so they need a little restoration work before you begin to decorate them. However, don't forget that bashes and dents add immeasurably to the character of a piece, so you don't want to get carried away and renovate the article so much that it looks brand-new.

As with the other jugs and coffee pots in this book, the first thing I did was to sand off all the flaking paint, inspect it for rust and act accordingly. In this case, there was a little rust so I painted on a rust remover and, when that had done its work and I had washed it off with white spirit (paint thinner), applied two coats of anti-rust paint. I had chosen a design that was a copy of a woollen tapestry worked in shades of blue, white and sand. I painted the inside of the jug in a pale blue, then followed all the other usual steps.

DENISE THOMAS

42

BLACK WASTEPAPER BIN

*E*veryone needs wastepaper bins but I think it's a *real shame that they're often so dull and boring, especially as it is easy to decorate them with découpage and transform them into works of art.*

I decided to make this wastepaper bin very sophisticated, with cherubs set against a jet black backround, but there is an alternative wastepaper bin for children on pages 76-7.

When varnishing objects like this bin, with its very visible and glossy background, it is important to make the finish as flawless as possible. That means you will have to keep an eagle eye out for drips of varnish, and sand the bin really well with fine wet and dry paper after you have applied between sixteen to eighteen layers of varnish. Make absolutely sure you have removed all specks of varnish dust with a clean cloth dipped in white spirit (paint thinner) before applying the penultimate coat of varnish, and then sand it down again. It is hard work but the gloss you achieve after the final coat of varnish has been applied is well worth it.

ABOVE AND LEFT *The designs of the decorated wastepaper bins you buy in the shops may not co-ordinate with your room but that is a problem easily solved if you are using découpage. For this bin I chose a sophisticated design in black and white, with a black background for the outside of the bin and a white one for the interior.*

FACING PAGE *This jug was painted in a deep blue to show off the lovely colours of the cut-outs and the interior was painted in a much paler blue to act as a contrast. I then followed my usual antiquing techniques to add age.*

MARY FOX

VICTORIAN BREAD PROVER

I have to admit that, in all my years of having been interested and involved in antiques, I had never seen a bread prover until I came across this one. That is one of the joys of working with antiques – every now and then you discover something new.

Whoever owned and used this bread prover would have placed it on the hob of their kitchen range, put the loaf tins (bread pans) full of dough inside it and replaced the lid. The heat rising up from the range would have made the dough rise and the lid of the prover would have ensured the atmosphere inside the box stayed suitably warm and steamy.

When I decorated this bread prover I followed exactly the same procedure as for the Victorian Military Campaign Box (see pages 82-3), but chose a very different decorative theme of ears of corn and wheat to act as a reminder of the prover's original purpose. I painted the outside of the prover a soldier red, but decided to decorate the inside in a lighter colour. I then mixed up some antique glaze (see page 104) and rubbed it into the surface, then wiped it off again, until I had achieved the effect I wanted. I then left it to dry. I know the varnishing process is lengthy, but it is well worth the effort when you can finally stand back and admire your work of art!

To make the decoration of this bread prover look suitably old I applied several coats of a pale blue emulsion (latex) paint for the base coat, criss-crossing the brush strokes to give an uneven and linen-like effect. The antique glaze which I applied next helped to darken the colour of the paint, and the many coats of varnish added a warm glow.

44

Two Edwardian Jugs

*F*or these two jugs I decided to get away from flower and bird motifs and chose animals instead. Working with découpage has meant I've collected some lovely old prints and, when I looked through them I found pictures of squirrels and other woodland animals that I thought would be ideal, so had them colour-photocopied.

The most important preliminary step with old enamel jugs is to rub off any flaking paint, remove any rust and prevent its return with one or two coats of anti-rust paint, leaving it to dry between applications. Now choose your base colour in emulsion (latex) – I used a pale green, and applied several coats criss-crossed over each other to create the effect of age. When the final coat was dry, I painted on a coat of gum water and allowed it to dry thoroughly, then carefully applied another coat of the pale green emulsion, taking care not to over-lap the strokes as that will remove the gum water. If this should happen (and I can assure you it sometimes does!), don't panic, just leave it to dry

and then fill in the gap with a blob of emulsion.

When the emulsion was dry, I rubbed in some antique glaze and then wiped it off, sealed the surface with a coat of matt (flat) varnish and left it to dry thoroughly. I then glued on the cut-outs and sealed them, as they were photocopies. When the surface was dry I applied the first of the twenty coats of matt varnish, followed by the craqueleur. After it had dried I went over it with a hair-drier to bring out the crackled effect. I rubbed in more of the antique glaze with a cloth and brushed it into all the places that were difficult to reach, then rubbed off the excess carefully, to leave some patches darker than others to create the right aged and dusty look. Finally, I varnished it.

These jugs were rather battered when I found them, but I wouldn't have dreamed of smoothing out the dents because they add to the character of the jugs. The last thing you want to do is make your découpaged antique look like a brand-new reproduction!

DENISE THOMAS

LARGE GREEN DEED BOX

*L*ike so many other pieces in this book, this deed box was found at a boot fair. I was very fortunate that it was in quite a good state of repair and not badly dented or misshapen. Don't buy boxes if their handles are missing or their lids don't fit.

One of the nicest features of this box is the old brass clasp which shone wonderfully after I had cleaned and polished it. I renovated and decorated this deed box in the usual way, rubbing off all the old paint before treating it for rust. I wanted the deed box to look its age, so painted it with pale green emulsion (latex), using cross-over brush strokes to give a suitably antique appearance. When the paint was dry I applied my antique glaze. You will see that I overlapped the cut-outs for an informal effect, and arranged them so they draped over the lid and around the sides of the box. When the glue for the cut-outs had completely dried and I'd removed all visible traces of it, I applied another coat of antique glaze, followed by a craqueleur, to give it as much authenticity as possible. After that came the long varnishing process, followed by a polish with good-quality beeswax.

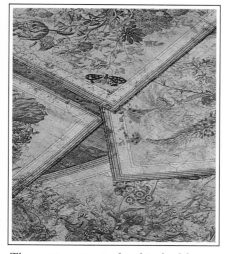

The pretty cut-outs for this deed box came from an old calendar which I had kept long after its year had ended – as you grow more fascinated by découpage you'll become reluctant to throw anything away. The pictures are beautiful eighteenth-century illustrations of seasonal plants and flowers.

DENISE THOMAS

DENISE THOMAS

Large Tin Travelling Trunk

W̲hen I found this trunk it had its original brass lock but, alas, no key to fit it. Sometimes that isn't a problem because you can unscrew the whole lock inside the lid and take it to a locksmith to have a new key cut but that wasn't possible for this trunk because the lock was riveted in place. However, the original sliding brass clips still worked so all was not lost. I liked the shape of this trunk and saw it as a really nice piece of antique furniture.

This trunk was covered with quite a lot of rust, so the first step was to remove it with a good rust remover, followed by a coat of anti-rust paint. I then applied two coats of soldier-red emulsion (latex). Having applied a coat of varnish and let it dry I glued on the cut-outs. As the trunk had an overall pattern on the lid I didn't wish to use any more cut-outs on the sides, so I decided to stencil some fleurs-de-lis and lions rampant on them

instead. To do this, I cut out the required shapes from a stiff piece of cardboard and used it as my stencil, with yellow emulsion (latex) paint on my stencil brush. When the stencils had dried I painted the inside of the trunk.

I applied two coats of varnish, letting the first one dry completely but waiting only until the second one was slightly tacky before painting on a coat of craqueleur. Having gone over it with a hairdrier when it was dry to bring out all the cracks, I rubbed on some antique glaze and wiped it off to leave light and dark patches, then left it to dry.

Then it was time to varnish, varnish, varnish. Finally, I gave the trunk a good rub with wax polish and marvelled, once again, at how rewarding it is to convert what was just an old black trunk into a beautiful decorative object.

This travelling trunk was not only decorated with cut-out images but also fleurs-de-lis and lions rampant which I stencilled around the sides using yellow paint. Although it looked very bright at first I knew the antique glaze and coats of varnish would tone it down.

DENISE THOMAS

FLORAL DEED BOX

*T*his deed box has a very similar shape to the
Ladies' Deed Box, but I decorated it in an
*entirely different way to show how similar objects can
be treated with a variety of découpage effects.*

I discovered this deed box when helping a friend to
clear out their cellar and swiftly realized what

could be done with it. Luckily it was in very good
condition so only had to be cleaned and rust-
proofed before I started on the découpage. I gave it
two base coats of light green emulsion (latex),
painting them on with cross-over strokes to give an
aged appearance, then a layer of antique glaze
when the paint was dry. I then glued on the cut-

52

If you compare the decorations on this deed box with the other boxes shown in this book you will get some idea of what a versatile craft découpage can be, and I hope will be suitably inspired to create your own découpage designs.

outs in the usual way, followed by two preliminary coats of varnish, the craqueleur and more antique glaze. On this piece it is easy to see the areas where I left on the antique glaze to make the piece look old and worn – in the crevices around the lid, around the handles and following the grain of the brush strokes. After that, of course, came the usual twenty or so coats of varnish, taking care not to let any drips form on the handles or rim.

——————— WILLIAM MORRIS TEA CADDY ———————

*W*hen tea was first drunk in Europe and America it was so expensive and precious that it was often locked away in special tea caddies for safe keeping. Today, those tea caddies can fetch good prices as antiques, and many are very beautiful in their original undecorated form. I loved the rounded top of this wooden tea caddy and decided it would make an excellent container for cards, with the score pads and pencils stored in the little box underneath.

The technique for varnishing a box is slightly different from the other projects in this book, because it is a good idea to varnish the rim and top edges first (in other words, around the hinges and the lip of the box). When they are thoroughly dry, put your hand inside the box and, using your hand as a turntable, varnish each exterior side of the box in turn. When you have varnished all four sides,

place the tea caddy on a tall object that is narrower than the box, so the varnished edges don't touch anything, and leave to dry. When every side of the box is thoroughly dry, varnish the top and leave to dry. Continue to build up the coats of varnish, applying them in this order so there won't be any drips on the sides or the top.

When you have completed all the varnishing and have applied a finishing coat of polish, you are ready to line the inside of the tea caddy. Place the box on a large piece of paper and draw around its base and sides – these outlines will act as your paper patterns. Place them on pieces of felt (or whichever fabric you are using for the lining) and cut them out, making them slightly smaller all around than the pencil outline. Carefully glue them on to the inside of the tea caddy, using a latex adhesive, press them in place then leave to dry.

I found this wooden tea caddy at a boot fair, and it was in surprisingly good condition – all it needed was a thorough clean with white spirit (paint thinner) to remove any polish and grease, then a rub-down with some fine wet and dry sandpaper. I did apply an undercoat but it wasn't really necessary. After it had dried I painted on a base coat of black emulsion (latex). Black is a very good colour for showing off découpage and, as I had chosen a bright William Morris design of flowers and leaves, I wanted them to stand out well from their background.

MARY FOX

BLUE JEWELLERY BOX

*F*inding boxes with their original brass locks and *keys is always a bonus, and so I was delighted when I found this one. All that was missing was its ring tray, but it still had its original satin lining.*

When I found it, this box was covered in a thin leather which had definitely seen better days, so I decided to paint it. Some of the pieces were hanging off in little tatters, so I sanded them all and also sanded down a few snags in the leather, then started to decorate the box. I chose a mid-blue emulsion (latex) paint for my base colour but applied several more coats than I would do for a wooden or metal object, to cover the leather properly.

I wanted the box to look exotic, so chose some beautiful pictures of birds, butterflies and flowers point where the lid and the base meet and glue the two pieces on the box so they flow together. The finished effect will be like that of a picture, rather than just having cut-outs dotted about at random.

I decided against crackling the box, so just gave it a coat of antique glaze instead, allowing plenty of time for it to dry thoroughly. Then came the lengthy process of applying my many coats of varnish, followed by a good buffing with antique polish. The finishing touch was to glue a piece of blue felt on the underside of the box, so it wouldn't scratch any wooden surface it might stand on.

DENISE THOMAS

It is easy to paint leather but, if you decide to decorate an old jewellery box like this one lined with satin or silk, do make sure you don't splash any paint on the fabric as it will be very difficult, or even impossible, to remove.

for my cut-outs which I thought would look very striking against the blue background. When decorating a box like this it is always effective to make the motifs flow from the lid to the base – if you look at the photograph showing the front of the box you will see that the branch on the left-hand side starts on the lid and flows down to the base of the box. This is easy to do – just choose a long cut-out and move it around until you're happy with its position, then carefully cut it in half at the

MARY FOX

———— FLORENTINE TABLE AND TRAY ————

I decorated both these objects with the same cut-outs, partly because I think the Florentine pattern is so beautiful and partly because I wanted to make the tray, which is modern, and the table, which is old, match.

Flowers work particularly well in découpage, but they do call for extra care when cutting out the shapes because if you stop concentrating you can easily slice through a petal or cut off the bottom of a leaf or stem by accident.

This tray was made from MDF (medium-density fibreboard). It is an excellent material for découpage as it is both firm and smooth, so needs no preliminary treatment. Firstly I sanded down the sides and surface of the tray, then applied a coat of undercoat and let it dry. This tends to bring up a certain amount of fluff, so I sanded it down until the surface was smooth again. I have no idea why this happens but have learnt to accept it – some MDF is worse than others. When I had a perfectly smooth top I applied three coats of a

tracing paper and draw around its outline with a pencil. Cut out the shape with a pair of scissors, cutting just inside the pencil lines, then use this paper as a pattern to cut out the piece of felt. Glue the felt in place with PVA adhesive (white craft glue) and leave to dry.

I discovered the table when I was sorting through my mother's effects. When I first examined it properly I toyed with the idea of simply découpaging the natural wood and then varnishing over it. However, after I'd cleaned off the original varnish the little table looked so battered and dejected that I realized I'd have to paint and découpage it in the usual way. I gave it a base coat of black paint and then decorated it with more of the Florentine cut-outs. The table now has a new lease of life in my conservatory.

good-quality black emulsion (latex) paint and allowed it to dry thoroughly.

I thought it would be effective to decorate the outer part of the tray this time, unlike the Parrot Tray (see page 62), and leave the centre plain. Because I had plenty of flower and leaf cut-outs I decided to make each half of the design a virtual reversed mirror image of the other one, although if you look closely you'll see that the decorations on the two long sides do vary to create extra interest.

When decorating a tray it is important to cover its base with felt so there is no danger of scratching the furniture. Place the tray on a large sheet of

This table and tray go very well together and have earned many compliments since I made them. It can be very attractive to make objects match in this way, especially if they will be used together.

VICTORIAN CANDLESTICKS

Candlesticks look wonderful when they've been decorated with découpage, and you can vary the design and paint colour according to the décor of your dining or sitting room. These candlesticks also make good presents for Christmas or birthdays.

When choosing cut-outs for a small delicate object such as a candlestick it is important to get the scale right – you don't want to smother the article with huge cut-outs but equally you don't want to decorate it with tiny motifs that get lost after you've applied your many coats of varnish.

I found a dramatic flower and grape design for these candlesticks, and followed all the usual découpage processes. You will see that I positioned some of the cut-outs to drape over the sides of the candlestick bases – this makes the leaves and tendrils of the flowers look much more realistic.

DENISE THOMAS

LADIES' DEED BOX

Here is yet another trophy from a boot fair! It is well worth suffering the vagaries of the weather to attend these fairs because you can pick up some marvellous objects if you are able to see their potential through the usual years of neglect and wear and tear. In fact, that is half the fun of découpage.

DENISE THOMAS

For this box I thought I'd follow a different method of découpage for a change and use one large print instead of several small ones. That can be difficult to do successfully because, once it is wet with glue, the paper can stretch and go into creases when you try to stick it in place, and you must also ensure you place the image in exactly the right position on the object you are decorating.

When the image is in place you must be extremely careful that all the glue has been pushed out from the centre to the edges, and there are no creases or lumps to spoil the effect.

Both of these projects have been given dark backgrounds to make the maximum impact and show off their cut-outs as much as possible.

——— FRUIT BOWL ———

*T*his bowl came from Kenya and was hand-carved, so therefore has a very interesting shape because it is not evenly cut. I wanted to decorate it in a way that would enhance its shape.

The bowl was covered in a simple form of varnish, so I had to lightly sand it down. As I had decided to turn it into a fruit bowl I chose a green emulsion (latex) paint for the base coat and painted it on the inside and outside of the bowl.

While the paint was drying I chose and cut out illustrations of a number of different fruits and vegetables. As the bowl is curved it is much more difficult than normal to glue the cut-outs in place because they have to stretch and also to shrink to fill the curves. Because the cut-outs overlap each other, glueing them in place is a very slow process as you have to let each piece dry thoroughly before applying the next one and if you discover an air bubble or a piece that is not stuck down properly you will have enormous problems cutting through several layers of cut-out to find the culprit.

Varnishing a bowl can take longer than a flat object because there are two sides to varnish and it is not possible to do both at the same time.

MARY FOX

MARY FOX

Parrot Tray

*T*rays are very popular découpage articles, perhaps because they combine usefulness with unique decorations. You can hunt around for old trays in need of renovation, or you could do as I did and have a number of trays made specially for you from MDF (medium-density fibreboard). This is an excellent material for trays because it is solid and smooth.

This parrot tray was made after I had discovered the joys of colour photocopying. However, it must be said that although colour photocopying is great in that you don't lose your original prints it is an expensive process. One good way of making the most of a colour photocopy is to choose illustrations with plenty going on in them, so you can use a small section of each print for each item, or use a little from one print and a bit from another – that is half the fun of découpage. In this case, however,

I just used one illustration and treated it in the usual way. When using MDF, don't forget to sand it down well after the undercoat has dried.

I always back my trays with felt in a contrasting colour, because it really finishes them off nicely and means they are less likely to scratch furniture. You can do this in exactly the same way as for the table mats (see pages 16-17).

I always cover the bottom of my trays with a piece of felt, in a matching colour, to ensure they don't scratch furniture when placed on it.

MARY FOX

CANDLESTICK

Candlesticks shaped like this one, whether old or new, are easily found in a variety of shops. For this project I bought a new candlestick but wanted to decorate it in a way that suited its traditional shape.

Although the candlestick was new and didn't need any preliminary restoration work, it still had to be sanded down with fairly coarse sandpaper to roughen the surface and provide a good key for the paint. After washing down the candlestick with white spirit (paint thinner) to remove all the dust and any grease from my fingers, I applied an undercoat and then mixed up a pink top coat using emulsion (latex) paint and acrylic paints.

After that, I followed the usual découpage processes, but had to be very careful when it came to varnishing the handle. Drips can easily gather inside handles, in which case you should leave that

coat of varnish to dry thoroughly and then sand down the offending blobs with fine grade wet and dry sandpaper, wipe over with white spirit and continue applying the coats of varnish. After the sixteenth coat of varnish had hardened I sanded down the whole candlestick with a small piece of wet and dry sandpaper, then washed it down with a clean cloth and white spirit. To finish off, I applied a coat of satin varnish which I sanded down after it had dried thoroughly, then wiped it down again and finally applied a coat of gloss varnish.

Although I decorated the saucer part of this candlestick with cut-outs of flowers, I didn't want to use them for the central piece so chose small strips of the ribbon cut-outs instead.

TARTAN BUCKET

*O*ne of the most interesting and exciting lessons I have learned from working with découpage is to think carefully before throwing anything away, because découpage can easily transform battered old objects into works of art in their own right. You will find many antiques in this book that have been given the découpage treatment, but there are also projects using everyday household items and even some objects that have been thrown out as rubbish by other people!

It is very important, when restoring an old object, to retain its original character and not do such a good job on it that it looks brand-new. To begin work on this bucket, I rubbed off all the flaking paint with a wire brush but left the surface slightly bumpy to enhance the bucket's antique appearance. I then rubbed down the bucket with a sheet of coarse sandpaper and immersed it in water to see if there were any holes (indicated by tell-tale air bubbles), which I repaired with car filler. After the filler had dried and I had roughly sanded down these patches (again, trying to keep the surface slightly lumpy), I gave the bucket two coats of rust-proof paint. It is better to apply two thin coats of this primer rather than one thick one. I allowed the primer to dry thoroughly, then applied at least two coats of emulsion (latex) paint in the base colours – a rich bottle green for the outside of the bucket and a bright scarlet for the inside. I then painted on a suitable tartan pattern, to complement the figures of the Scottish soldiers, using dark brown and green acrylic paints, and left the bucket to dry before glueing on the cut-outs and beginning to apply the many coats of varnish.

This tartan bucket is a good example of the way découpage can give a new lease of life to an object that has definitely seen better days. I bought a job lot of these buckets at a boot sale and saw, beyond their rust, flaking paint and sad appearance, that they offered plenty of scope for some exciting découpage treatments. Because there were several buckets to decorate I could experiment with them, so gave some a plain coat of paint (as in the step-by-step sequence on pages 14-15), and painted others in this tartan pattern before adding the decorations. The linking theme for all the buckets, however, was the soldiers.

DENISE THOMAS

Military Despatch Case

*T*his is a rather unusual piece, and is the sort of object I love working on. I don't know much about its history and can only guess it could have been a Civil Service despatch case or perhaps used by a bank clerk. Who knows? However, I decided to give it an importance it probably didn't have originally, so chose the Royal Engineers as my theme and hunted for some suitable decorations.

I followed the usual process in decorating this despatch case – sanding it down to remove any flaking paint, applying two coats of a rust-proof paint, followed by the undercoat and then the top-coat in my chosen colour of black. The insignia of the Royal Engineers was so decorative that I didn't want to detract from its impact, so positioned it, with its two soldiers, underneath the lock on the front of the box. However, I did decorate the lid and other sides with cut-out figures of soldiers with gun carriages, horses and carts.

I decorated the inside of the case in a cheery shade of red to match the jackets of the soldiers, and aged the interior and exterior of the case with antique glaze. The edges of the case were metal, so I rubbed lots of antique gold cream into them with my finger and then rubbed it off with some steel wool, taking care to create an aged and worn look with some parts shinier than others. I left it to dry thoroughly before applying the first of my twenty or so coats of varnish, and finished it off in the usual way with wax polish. As you can see in the photograph, this case now shines beautifully.

The photographs of this Military Despatch Case show the way I decorated it but they also show that I made no attempt to smooth out the dents and uneven surface that it had when I found it. The only restoration work I did on the case was to remove all the flaking paint and give it two coats of a good-quality rust-proof paint. I also gave the metal fittings, such as the handle and attractive lock, a thorough polish so they would shine nicely (but not garishly) and look good against the black background of the case.

DENISE THOMAS

Fire (place) Screen

*T*his screen was commissioned by a friend who wished it to match a fire bucket I had previously découpaged for her and also her marble fireplace. You can either search out an old fire (place) screen that will be easy to decorate, or you can use a new one, as I did, from MDF (medium-density fibreboard). According to your carpentry skills, you can either make it yourself or ask someone else to do it for you.

MDF is a man-made product with a very smooth surface, so all I had to do was rub it down with some sandpaper to provide a key for the paint. I then wiped it down well with a clean cloth dipped in white spirit (paint thinner) to remove all traces of dust and applied an undercoat to both sides of the screen. After it had dried, I sanded it down again to remove the strange fluffing that always appears when MDF receives its first coat of paint, and then mixed up the base coat. For this, I chose the same terracotta colour that I had used for the friend's bucket, using an emulsion (latex) paint mixed with acrylic paints until I had the colour I wanted.

While waiting for the second coat of base colour to dry, I started cutting out the motifs. I had chosen a paper of a very famous medieval tapestry, known as The Lady and the Unicorn, which was ideal for this fire screen because its wide shape allowed me to put in plenty of detail from the tapestry. I cut out the main image of the beautiful tent with the couple standing in front of it, plus the unicorn on the couple's left and the lion on their right. As you can see, this central image is actually one large cut-out, so it was a time-consuming and fiddly process to cut around all the outlines.

I wanted to keep the wonderful trees, with their stately yet simple shapes, so cut them out too (and then had to trim them to fit on to the screen), plus the dogs in the foreground of the screen and all the other elements you can see, and then spent a long time carefully arranging all the cut-outs in place until I was happy with them. Glueing the cut-outs in place took a long time because it was very important to ensure all the air bubbles and lumps of glue had been smoothed out from under all the images, but especially the large central one.

When I was sure all the cut-outs were in the right place and were free of lumps, bumps and air bubbles, I left them to dry, then checked their edges to ensure they were all stuck down. After that, I

followed the usual processes of applying all those endless but necessary coats of varnish, and sanded down the surface well after painting on the eighteenth coat, before applying the final two coats of varnish.

The finishing touch was to give the screen a handle so it could be carried around, so I drilled suitably sized holes through the back of the screen and screwed on a small brass handle.

This fire (place) screen was designed for an adult, but I have also découpaged these screens for children's nurseries and turned taller ones into purely decorative objects. These fire screens are very useful but do take care not to place them too near to an open fire because you don't want them to catch alight.

Child's Toy Box

*M*ost parents of young children are well aware of the benefits of giving their offspring a toy box, because it is wonderful to have somewhere to store all those toys and games that otherwise seem to spread in all directions until they have taken over the house.

I decorated the box in the usual way, and began by rubbing off the loose paint with a wire brush and then applying a coat of anti-rust paint. In this case it was a preventative measure rather than a treatment so I only used one coat, but if the box you find already has spots of rust you should use two coats to make sure you have killed it off completely. Because I was using cut-outs of old-fashioned toys I wanted the box to look in keeping so painted on the base colour with criss-cross strokes.

After that, I worked in the usual way, sticking on my cut-outs and leaving them to dry thoroughly before applying my first coat of varnish. To create the right antique effect I painted on a coat of craqueleur when the second coat of varnish was still slightly tacky, then encouraged the cracks to form with a hair-drier when the craqueleur was dry. After that, I made up my usual antique glaze and mixed it with a little raw umber artists' oil paint before rubbing it on and off again in the usual way. You can also add imitation fly spots at this stage if you wish (see page 105). After leaving the craqueleur to dry for several days I began applying all my coats of varnish.

The final stage was to polish the inside and outside of the box with beeswax. I always use a matt (flat), rather than a gloss, varnish because I think you get a much better and finer sheen with beeswax polish than with any polyurethane varnish.

This toy box is an old metal box that I found on a trip to a boot fair and I particularly liked the metal plaque underneath the lock that bears the manufacturer's name. If you don't have children but find a container like this you could turn it into a blanket box instead.

DENISE THOMAS

— PENCIL OR PAINTBRUSH HOLDER —

*T*his pencil or paintbrush holder just goes to show that you can use all sorts of articles for découpage. I can never bear to throw away large Dijon mustard pots, because there always seems to be another use for them. Decorating them with découpage is very simple because they are made of pottery, so don't need to be treated for rust or woodworm.

The surface of most of these mustard pots is shiny, so you will have to sand it down to provide a key for the paint to grip. As with most of the projects in this book, it is a good idea to wear a face mask while sanding down as it is only too easy to breathe in the fine dust. After you have brushed off the dust the pot is ready to be decorated.

You can paint and découpage a mustard pot in any colour you wish, perhaps making it bright and cheerful for a child, or giving it a dark base coat and so creating a much more sophisticated pot for an adult. The finished effect will also be influenced by the style of cut-outs you use. For this pot, intended for a child, I chose a wonderfully vivid cobalt blue for the base coat, then applied cut-outs in simple primary colours. As children love personalized objects which have been made specially for them, you could use letters that spell out their name or pictures of objects they particularly like, such as teddy bears or steam engines. To make the pot extra shiny, I applied about sixteen coats of varnish and then rubbed the surface of the pot in a circular motion with a sheet of fine wet and dry sandpaper until the surface was completely smooth. I wiped away all the dust with a cloth dipped in white spirit (paint thinner), applied another coat of varnish and sanded it again when it was dry, wiped it clean and then applied the final coat of varnish.

To turn these mustard pots into bedside lights, drill a hole for the cord in the base of one of the sides and drill another hole in the centre of the original cork lid. Decorate this lid to match the rest of the pot, then attach a light fitting (holder) and cord. It will look very attractive and is sturdy enough not to be knocked over easily.

This old Dijon mustard pot has been decorated for use by a child, but of course it would be easy to choose different cut-outs and perhaps another background colour to make a pencil holder for an adult.

MARY FOX

75

MARY FOX

TEDDY BEAR WASTEPAPER BIN

I enjoy making découpaged objects for children because of the bright colours and simple shapes that suit them so well, so decided it would be fun to make a wastepaper bin for a child's bedroom, decorated with teddy bears and balloons.

Unlike the Black Wastepaper Bin (see page 43), which is for adults and therefore rather elegant, I made this one very light-hearted and simple. Having painted it white, I glued on the cut-outs of the bears and balloons, making absolutely sure that I had pressed out all the air bubbles and lumps of glue before leaving them to dry. I then varnished the bin well, applying about eighteen coats before sanding down the varnish with wet and dry paper, followed by another coat of varnish, another sanding down and then the final coat of varnish. Children can really punish their belongings so it is essential to make sure any objects you have

découpaged for them are protected by plenty of coats of varnish to avoid too much damage.

If you talk nicely to the owner or manager of the local ice cream shop or parlour, they may let you have some of the old ice cream tubs which are perfect for converting into wastepaper bins. In fact, even old paint cans are suitable for turning into bins, provided you've gone through the time-consuming task of cleaning them thoroughly first! To do this, you will have to remove all the old paint thoroughly – use a little paint stripper followed by white spirit (paint thinner), for oil-based paints, and white spirit for emulsion (latex) paint. Clean well with hot soapy water and leave to dry.

When découpaging objects for children, such as a wastepaper bin like this one, it is essential to give them plenty of coats of varnish because of all the wear and tear they are bound to receive.

77

CHILD'S GREEN BOWLS

*A*ll sorts of household items can be decorated with découpage, including bowls, which look very good when adorned in this way. Because bowls are cheap to buy and quick to decorate they are good projects for beginners, although it could take a little practice to glue your cut-outs on to a curved surface – you'll find that some shapes work better than others.

I bought these bowls new and, because they were heavily varnished, had to sand them down well and then wash them with white spirit (paint thinner) before I applied the undercoat. Because I was going to make these bowls for a child I wanted to paint them in a vivid colour, so mixed up a base coat of bright green paint using green emulsion (latex) and acrylic paints.

After applying two layers of base coat to each bowl and letting them dry thoroughly, I was ready to stick on my cut-outs. In contrast with the rest of the projects in this book, I had decided to create my own images for these bowls, so drew and painted various childlike objects, cut them out and sprayed each one with sealer.

It is sometimes difficult to make cut-outs adhere to a curved surface, so I always decide exactly where I will be putting them and then finely sand the paint in that place – it gives a good key for the glue and helps to ensure the cut-out is firmly fixed in position. The moisture from the glue will help you to smooth out any wrinkles in the cut-out caused by the curved surface, but do be patient otherwise you could tear the paper. Another potential problem with curved surfaces is leaving small bubbles of glue in the centre of the cut-out, so take care to smooth down the cut-outs well while the glue is wet to ensure this doesn't happen.

When they were thoroughly dry, I removed all the surplus glue from the bowls and checked that all the edges were stuck down well, with no air bubbles lurking to spoil the finished effect, before beginning to apply my many coats of varnish. I sanded the bowl down after the eighteenth coat of varnish had dried, then applied another coat of varnish and sanded it again before painting on the final coat of gloss varnish for extra shine.

It can take a little practice to glue cut-outs to curved surfaces successfully, but sanding down the exact place where they will be glued can help to hold them firm.

MARY FOX

GREEN BISCUIT (CRACKER) BARREL

Découpage works just as well on modern objects and pieces of furniture as it does on old and antique ones, as you can see from this biscuit (cracker) barrel which I have decorated in green.

To prepare the barrel, I removed all the old paint with paint stripper – this is best done in either a well-ventilated room or, preferably, in the fresh air. In either case you should wear a mask and gloves, and wash off any splashes immediately with plenty of cold water. I removed the paint stripper with white spirit (paint thinner), being particularly careful to eliminate all traces of it from inside the container. When it was dry, I applied a layer of undercoat to the inside and outside of the barrel and both sides of its lid, then painted the box and lid a vibrant jade green. When the second coat had dried I carefully glued on all the cut-outs.

It was then time to begin painting on the coats of varnish – I applied about sixteen in all. When the final coat was dry I rubbed it over with some wet and dry sandpaper in a circular motion. The lid didn't have a handle, so I made a cross of masking tape across the centre and, with a small drill, bored a hole. I then peeled off the masking tape and applied two more coats of varnish to both sides of the lid. I sanded it down again with a piece of fine-grade wet and dry sandpaper, wiped off the dust and applied the final two coats of varnish, then screwed the small gilt handle on to the lid.

When giving your object a highly lacquered finish you must make sure there is no dust on the object or work surface before applying the final two coats of varnish.

MARY FOX

DENISE THOMAS

————— Victorian Military Campaign Box —————

*I*t is great fun hunting in shops and sale rooms for old chests and boxes and I was very lucky to find this Victorian military campaign box in such good condition, and even containing its original ink bottles and key. I therefore decided to preserve its character and emphasize its army background, so chose military figures for my decorative theme.

Before decorating the box I removed all the flaking paint with a wire brush, then sanded down the surface with some wet and dry sandpaper. I then applied two coats of anti-rust paint, followed by three coats of white emulsion (latex) paint, which I painted on with rough brush strokes to get a cross-hatched effect. I mixed up my antique glaze, then

As it was a military box I wanted to decorate it with military figures, so cut them out and glued them on in the usual way. After that, I painted on two coats of varnish, followed by the craqueleur. Then I mixed up another glaze, from equal parts of raw linseed oil, white spirit (paint thinner) and polyurethane varnish, with a squeeze of raw umber artists' oil paint and a tiny amount of black. I rubbed this into the cracks and then rubbed it off, leaving the glaze in the cracks, crevices and corners which would naturally have become darker in colour over the years.

After waiting a couple of days for the antique glaze to dry completely, I began the important process of varnishing, and finished the box with a good beeswax polish.

When ageing articles with antique glaze, which involves rubbing it into the cracks and crevices, I can only suggest that you look carefully at real antiques to see how they appear after years of use and general wear and tear — copying that look is the art of antiquing.

mixed a small amount of this glaze with a squeeze of raw umber, burnt sienna and yellow ochre artists' oil paints, plus a touch of black oil paint. This gives a good rich colour, and looks like leather when it has dried. I brushed it on then wiped some off with a clean rag, merging the colours and areas of light and shade together until I was happy with the way it looked. I let this glaze dry thoroughly for at least twenty-four hours.

Floral Mirror

*T*his mirror is a good example of what can be done with a utilitarian object – the découpage has turned what was a very basic mirror into something that is attractive yet still usable.

I found this mirror at a boot fair and it looked in such a state that it was hardly surprising no one else had bought it. However, I could see that it had potential because, although the frame looked awful the mirror itself was in good condition.

Having taken the mirror home I started to remove all the old paint and varnish from the frame. When I had stripped it right back I could see there were various scratches and holes, so I filled them all and then sanded them down. This mirror has a very narrow frame so there wasn't much space for the decorations and I had to choose a small design. I eventually decided on a delicate floral pattern around each corner, with the pieces linked together to look like little garlands and stop them seeming bitty. I have had plenty of opportunity to review my work on this mirror because it now adorns the dressing room of a small beauty shop that I frequent!

Although the surround of this mirror was in a dreadful state when I bought it, the mirror itself was perfectly serviceable — there is little point in buying a mirror that has lost its silver backing unless, of course, it is so old or so beautiful that you don't mind. If you can't find a suitable mirror you could use a picture or photograph frame instead, and both of these make marvellous presents for birthdays, Christmas or other special occasions.

MARY FOX

MILK CHURN

*M*ilk *churns have been hand-painted and given the découpage treatment many, many times, but when I was walking around my nephew's farm and spotted several churns lying there looking very sad I decided to join the club!*

Removing all the rust and various other deposits that had accumulated over the years was quite a challenge, and is certainly a job that is best done outside because of the terrible mess it makes. After scrubbing the churn I applied two coats of rust remover. I then painted both the inside and outside with an anti-rust paint – always wear a mask while doing this, preferably outside, because the paint fumes are very unpleasant. I applied two coats of this paint because the milk churn had suffered a lot of harsh treatment.

After the anti-rust paint had dried (which it does very quickly), I painted the outside with two coats of emulsion (latex) in the base colour. Having stuck the cut-outs in position with a wallpaper paste I washed away the surplus glue and started the long process of varnishing. In this case I used a gel varnish because I didn't want it to drip, and it also gives a very good cover so doesn't require the usual twenty coats. After about ten coats I rubbed the varnish down with a fine piece of wet and dry sandpaper, then applied a final coat of varnish to which I had added a tiny amount of raw umber paint to give a warm glow.

When I found this milk churn it was thick with dirt and cleaning it took some time. Firstly I turned the garden hose on the inside and outside of it to remove the worst of the surface dirt, then scrubbed with a wire brush. When the churn was clean and dry, I painted the interior with a rust remover and left it to dry. Not all the rust had gone so I applied a second coat, then washed down the churn with white spirit (paint thinner) before applying an anti-rust paint.

MARY FOX

BEIGE BOWL

*B*owls *are very satisfying objects to work on, because I like their curved shapes and the challenge they present when trying to glue on the cut-outs without creating any wrinkles or air bubbles.*

Like the child's green bowls, this beige bowl was new when I bought it, so I had to sand off the heavy varnish that had been applied to it before I was able to begin work.

I mixed a suitable emulsion (latex) with some acrylic paint to get the right colour, then applied two coats of it to the bowl. After the second coat had dried, I arranged the cut-outs on the bowl and, when I was sure of their positions, sanded down the paint in those places, to ensure the glue would adhere well. After glueing them in position, and checking rigorously for any trapped air bubbles or blobs of glue, I left the cut-outs to dry and then began to apply the varnish. I wanted the bowl to have a highly lacquered finish, so sanded down the eighteenth coat with some fine wet and dry paper, wiped off the white scum that formed, applied a coat of satin varnish and sanded it again before carefully painting on the final coat of satin varnish.

When looking for some decorative motifs for another project one day I found these images of autumnal-coloured fruits and decided they would look good on a bowl with a beige background.

MARY FOX

Materials
Equipment and Techniques

*Even a postcard can inspire a
découpage design.*

Perhaps one of the best aspects of découpage is that
you don't have to spend a lot of money on all the
materials you will need. The basic requirements are
very simple, although you will soon discover there are
refinements you can make if you wish but these are
not essential by any means.

When you first begin découpaging, all you will
need are a pair of very fine cuticle scissors or a scalpel
knife with a very sharp blade, an object to découpage,
emulsion (latex) or oil paint, pictures, sealer, glue,
varnish and a few brushes. Each separate stage of
découpaging will be explained in this chapter, either
with step-by-step illustrations
or clear instructions.

MATERIALS AND EQUIPMENT

You only need a few basic materials when you begin découpage work, and here is a list of the most important items you will need.

Acrylic paints

You can use these to add colour and tone to your emulsion (latex) paint. They can also be used to add highlights or lowlights to cut-outs and to cover up any mistakes made in cutting out or sanding later on. Always mix with water and test the colours before applying them to your object. Acrylic paints are quick-drying.

Paints

You can either use emulsion (latex) or oil-based paints to cover your article before you begin to découpage it, but an oil-based paint does give a finer patina on wooden items which will be lacquered to a fine finish. If you are antiquing a piece your choice of paint will depend entirely on the glazes you will be using. When using gum water you must always paint with emulsion because it is the second coat of emulsion which acts with the gum water to create a peeled-paint effect.

Polishes

To finish off your découpaged article and achieve an immaculate finish you must polish it. To do this, you can make up a paste using rottenstone, which is a fine grey powder that can be bought from specialist shops. Mix it with vegetable or baby oil, or lemon essential oil. Rub it on with a clean soft cloth, or a clean old pair of tights (pantyhose) or stockings, using a circular movement, then buff with a soft duster (dust cloth) or flannel. You can use French chalk (talc) or even white flour instead of rottenstone if you wish. Sometimes, on a very fine lacquer finish, you can rub the varnished surface with the very finest wire (steel) wool, then rub in a good-quality beeswax or antique polish with a clean soft duster and leave for several hours before buffing it hard with another clean duster. Some polishes are available in different colours, so be careful to buy the right shade.

All découpaged articles should be kept polished, just as you would polish any other antique pieces of furniture you have in your house. By the same token it is vitally important never to leave them in direct sunlight or close to a heat source.

Primers

When working on tin, iron ware or enamelware, you must treat the surface with a good-quality rust remover followed by a primer. Some metal paint does not need a primer because it is incorporated in the paint.

To prime terracotta, which is extremely porous, you need to apply a sealer (see below) followed by one coat of varnish.

To prime old wooden furniture, you must treat it with woodworm remover. Check the piece for the tell-tale holes and squirt the woodworm killer into each one, even if you think the worm has long since departed. It could only be dormant, so take no risks. Do not fill the worm holes unless they are very large because that will destroy the antiquity of the piece.

Gesso is a very useful primer which can be used to create a smooth hard surface on which to work. Apply one coat of gesso and leave it to dry before applying the background paint. There are several well-known brands of gesso on the market.

Sealers

If you use colour photocopies or hand-painted designs for your cut-outs you will have to seal them after cutting them out. Print sealers can be bought in spray form from most good stationers' or office supply shops. There are three types to choose from – matt, flat or gloss. PVA adhesive (white craft glue), diluted one part glue to two parts water, acts as a sealer. Do not use shellac because it contains natural wax – varnish never works when applied over wax.

Varnishes

The range of well-known varnishes is increasing. You can apply either polyurethane or acrylic varnishes to découpaged objects, according to the effect you want. Polyurethane varnishes are available in matt (flat), semi-matt, satin and gloss finishes, and also in drip or non-drip. They tend to turn your article and cut-outs a darker colour than they were originally and they also yellow with age, so are essential when antiquing pieces. There are several good-quality acrylic varnishes on the market (these do not discolour) but they do tend to give a harder appearance to the finished article than polyurethane and so lose the effect of a polished sheen.

Equipment

You do not need much equipment for découpage work, but do make sure that the few items you do buy are of the best quality you can afford.

Cutting board

If you are going to cut out your images with a scalpel knife and not cuticle scissors (see below) you will need a good rubberized self-healing cutting board. Such boards are also used for stencilling and are available from art supply shops. They are expensive but invaluable when using a scalpel knife and stand up to a great deal of wear and tear. You can also use the white man-made acrylic chopping or carving boards that are sold in kitchen shops. They are very easy to clean if you place your cutouts on them when painting on the glue.

Lining (liner) paper

This can be bought in rolls from hardwear shops and wallpaper suppliers and is useful for covering your worktop and protecting it from spills and splashes. Tear off the required length and hold it in place with masking tape.

Masking tape

This is a cream-coloured sticky paper that is sold in rolls from art supply shops and some hardwear shops. It is available in a variety of widths. You can secure lining (liner) paper over your work surface with masking tape. Sometimes you will also need to tape it to the painted surface of your découpaged article, in which case it is advisable to stick it on to a piece of cloth first to remove most of the glue, otherwise it can pull off the paint.

Sandpaper

Sandpaper is available in a variety of grades, from extremely fine to very coarse, and you will need a good selection of each sort. You will need sand-paper for rubbing off any flaking paint and rust, for keying shiny surfaces so paint can grip them, for sanding between coats of varnish and for making good any repairs when something goes wrong. Always use a new piece of sandpaper each time rather than a piece that is already worn out. It is advisable to use wet and dry paper for sanding between coats of varnish because it does leave a smoother surface. Use fairly fine ordinary sandpaper when rubbing down any wood filler you have had to apply.

Scalpel knife

If you decide against using a pair of cuticle scissors to cut out your images you will need a scalpel knife instead. Scalpel knives and their blades are available from good art supply shops and pharmacies. When not in use, always keep the point of the scalpel blade protected by impaling it in a wine cork or something similar. The blades do become blunt, so have a good supply of replacements to hand because a blunt blade will tear your cut-outs. If you have children, it is essential to keep scalpel knives and blades out of their reach at all times.

Scissors

You will need two pairs – a large pair for cutting away the surplus paper around your cut-outs, and a very fine pair for your actual cutting, unless you decide to use a scalpel knife instead. Cuticle scissors are ideal because they have small curved blades and sharp points, but they can be difficult to find in shops. Never use them for cutting anything else or you will blunt them.

Surgical gloves

It is always advisable to work in a pair of surgical gloves, which are made of very fine transparent rubber, because otherwise you can stain your hands with paints and other chemicals. The gloves can be bought at most good chemists or pharmacies.

Wire (steel) wool

Sometimes you will need fine-grade wire (steel) wool for rubbing down surfaces and also applying polishes. It is available from most hardwear shops but do ask for the very fine, not coarse, grade.

SUITABLE ARTICLES FOR
DECOUPAGE

We would recommend that you begin your découpage work on an inexpensive flat object rather than something costly and complicated, just as you would learn to knit by making simple garments first before going on to create something more intricate and time-consuming.

Table mats are good articles to start with because they are flat and therefore easy to decorate. They will also help you to understand the principles of designing découpage – some people like to smother their articles with so much decoration that

91

These are just some of the items suitable for découpage.

fairs, junk (thrift) shops, jumble sales and anywhere else that you hope will offer rich pickings.

PAPERS, PRINTS, POSTCARDS —— AND PAINTINGS ——

When you start to search for objects to découpage you will also be looking for papers and other decorative images. You can use sheets of wrapping paper, although you must not sell any articles decorated with images that have been copyrighted by someone else – if you look carefully at the sheet of wrapping paper you will usually see a couple of lines of printing saying who designed the paper and who owns the copyright.

Some publishers produce books of black and white images specially intended to be re-used without any copyright problems. You can buy books of decorative borders, fancy or plain initials (very useful when personalizing an object for someone), flowers, animals and all sorts of other images as well. For more information, turn to the list of suppliers at the back of the book.

Prints

Another rich source of images is old prints, which are especially suitable for decorating antiques. The advent of colour photocopying means you don't have to cut up these prints if you want to use them. Libraries are often full of suitable books, or you may find some in second-hand shops. However, it must be said that colour photocopying can be quite pricey so, although it is a much better prospect than having to cut up one of your precious books (which you couldn't do at all, of course, if you had borrowed it from a library), it is still a good idea to be absolutely sure which prints you want to use before having them copied.

Postcards

Postcards or birthday cards can also be suitable, although the copyright rule may apply to them too. If the card is too thick to be applied direct to an object, you will have to peel off the backing carefully. This is a tricky process that neither of us have had much luck with, although we know other people who have succeeded with it.

Paintings

If you are very artistic and want to create your own

they look more like collages than objects decorated with a few cut-out images, but we both prefer to leave lots of the background showing. However, like all artistic ventures, this is purely a matter of taste and there is no right and wrong involved – it is up to you to discover your personal découpage style and then have fun developing it in whichever way suits you best.

Boxes, bowls, trays, jugs, mugs, casserole dishes, pots, tea urns and all sorts of other household items can be decorated, and you can also recall the history of découpage by decorating pieces of furniture, such as chests, chairs, tables, beds, mirrors, wardrobes, cupboard doors, stools and even finger plates and knobs for doors. In fact, virtually anything which has a relatively smooth surface can be decorated with découpage. You can even decorate large stones found on the beach and turn them into beautiful doorstops. Once you start looking for objects you will probably be amazed at the range of suitable items. Some of them may be found lurking at home at the backs of cupboards or in the attic, while others could be found in other people's cupboards or attics, as were some of the pieces in this book. You can also go shopping for suitable articles at boot

You can use all sorts of papers and prints as images.

it by soaking it in a dish of clean warm water for a few minutes and then carefully peeling the back off. Leave to dry on a sheet of clean blotting paper. An alternative method is to moisten the back of the print or paper with vinegar, but not soak it. Leave it for a minute or two and then rub the back of the image with your finger or a small piece of sponge until it has reached the required thinness. Both of these techniques depend on the quality of the print or paper concerned and sometimes it is just not possible. It doesn't matter if you have to use thick paper for découpage – it merely means you will have to use more coats of varnish than usual to submerge the picture into its surroundings.

PREPARATION AND PAINTING

You will need
Wire brush for removing rust
Anti-rust paint
Wire (steel) wool
Gesso and cheap brush
Wood filler
Water and vinegar or lemon juice
Brushes
Oil-based paint
Emulsion (latex) paint
Acrylic paint
Paint-colouring additives

images you can paint them before cutting them out. This is especially effective when découpaging objects intended for children, particularly if you paint the images in bright clear colours.

It is important, however, to link your decorative images with the history of the object to be découpaged. For example, when decorating a military chest you might want to use figures of old soldiers, or a ladies' hat box could be decorated with delicately coloured Victorian flowers. Quite often you will see antiques that have been decorated with modern images, thereby taking away their value and making them anachronisms that will never become antiques of the future.

Some of the objects you will be working on will probably be old and battered, and may therefore need some restoration work before you can begin to découpage them. Metal objects must be treated for rust, whether or not you can see any, because otherwise patches of rust can appear long after you have finished the découpage and will ruin the object's appearance. Although you want to make the object rust-free or, if it is wooden, free of woodworm, you don't want to do such a good job of restoring it that it looks brand-new. Instead, keep its character but remove any potential problems.

Personal items

As well as all these options you can also use very personal items, such as a wedding invitation decorated with a border of cut-out flowers for a tray for the bride and groom, either to celebrate their wedding or an anniversary. There are endless possibilities and you will have fun discovering them.

Peeling the back off thick paper

If your print or paper is too thick it is best to thin

Removing and preventing rust

Rub off any flaking paint and patches of rust with a wire brush, but don't rub off anything else or you will destroy the original character of the piece. Now, using a special brush which you keep for this purpose only, coat your article (inside and out) with a good-quality rust remover and leave it to dry thoroughly, then wash it down well with white spirit (paint thinner). You may have to apply a second coat of rust remover if the rust is very bad. Sometimes small holes can appear in the metal during this process but that is not a problem because you can fill them with an excellent filler which is made for car repairs and does the job perfectly. Allow the filler to dry and then sand it down with coarse sandpaper. Now you are ready to apply an anti-rust/undercoat preparation. It usually comes in two finishes, smooth or rough. Paint the object with a coat of it and leave to dry thoroughly. It is now ready for its base coat.

Removing old paint

If you are working on old furniture which has been painted, you must strip it down to the bare wood. Do this with a proprietary paint stripper and follow the manufacturer's instructions carefully. If possible, work outside and wear a face mask, goggles and gloves for protection. When you have stripped off all the paint, wash the article down with white spirit (paint thinner).

Checking for and preventing woodworm

If you are working on old furniture, you must check it for woodworm. Look for any holes and, if you find any, treat them with a proprietary woodworm killer by following the manufacturer's instructions. If the holes are very large or, indeed, if any lumps of the furniture are actually missing, you can use a good-quality wood filler to repair the damage. Normally, however, it adds to the antiquity and character of a piece to leave the woodworm holes unfilled (but definitely not untreated).

Removing old polish

If wooden objects haven't been painted then they have usually been polished. It is easier to sand them down if you remove the polish first, because otherwise the sandpaper can slip on the smooth surface. Wash down the object with a mixture of water and vinegar or lemon juice and leave to dry. Wrap a piece of sandpaper around a small block of wood, so you've got something to grip, and begin to sand down the object, working with the grain of the wood. When you are down to the bare wood, wash the entire object with white spirit (paint thinner). If you are working on chairs, tables and similar objects, don't forget to sand down the legs, cross-supports and backs.

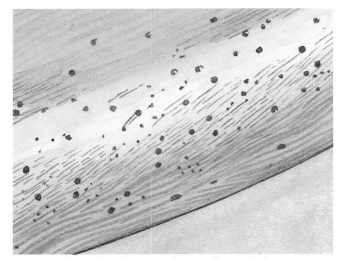
Inspect old wooden furniture for woodworm holes.

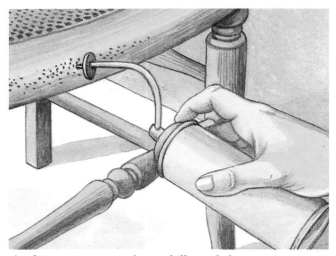
Apply proprietary woodworm killer to holes.

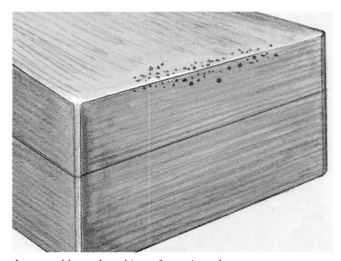
Inspect old wooden objects for serious damage.

Applying gesso

If your surface is rough or pitted it is a good idea to apply one coat of gesso, which will give a smooth finish. There are several acrylic versions of this on the market and they are available from good art supply shops.

Applying the undercoat and base coats

Once the surface of the object is smooth you can apply the undercoat, although this will not be necessary if you have used an anti-rust/undercoat (on metal) or gesso (on wood). You can use any muted colour for the undercoat, in either an emulsion (latex) or oil-based paint. Leave it to dry thoroughly, then mix up your base coat.

You can either use an emulsion paint for this or an oil-based paint, although if you use an emulsion you must seal it with a sparing coat of varnish before applying the cut-outs. You may find a paint that is the exact colour you want, or you can blend your own – add acrylic paint or powder pigment to emulsion, and artists' oils to oil-based paints. Use an egg beater to mix the powder or acrylic paints. Apply a couple of coats, letting the first one dry before applying the second. Seal the emulsion with a thin coat of varnish and leave to dry again. You are now ready to glue on your cut-outs.

CUTTING

You will need
Sealer (optional)
Ordinary scissors
Very small curved cuticle scissors
Scalpel knife and blades

One of the interesting points about this book is that it has been written by two people with totally different approaches to découpage – including two ways of cutting out images!

We will start this section with the method using cuticle scissors. These must be very sharp and very small, and never used for any purpose other than découpage (and certainly not the one for which they were intended). If they become blunt they can tear the paper and so ruin a design. The other method of cutting out uses a scalpel knife and self-healing cutting board.

Before starting to cut out your image using either scissors or scalpel it is a good idea to seal the picture. You don't need to do this with wrapping

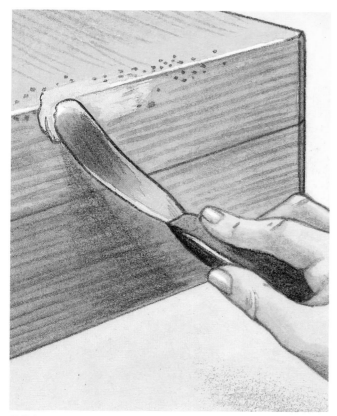

Fill large gaps or holes with wood filler.

Sand filler down well when it is dry.

paper, but it should certainly be done when using photocopies because otherwise their dyes may leach out into the varnish. There are a number of sealers on the market and your local art shop should be able to advise you on which one to buy.

Seal cut-outs with diluted PVA (white craft) glue.

Alternatively, spray with an aerosol sealer.

Seal wood before applying paint.

Cutting around the image

You are now ready to start cutting out your print or picture. First cut away all the surplus paper surrounding the image you require, using the ordinary scissors. However, do make sure you don't slice your way through an image that you might not want to use now but which would definitely be useful in the future! Leave only the heart of the print, but keep enough to hold without touching the actual image. You have now finished with the ordinary scissors for the time being.

Cutting out with cuticle scissors

Look carefully at the picture and start cutting all the paper away from the centre of the picture by pushing the point of the small cuticle scissors into the picture from above. When you have made a small hole, pull the scissors out and start cutting away from underneath the picture – this enables you to see where you are going, so only the points of the scissors are visible and you are able to cut around delicate flowers or along branches instead of accidentally slicing through them and so ruining them. Hold the scissors fairly loosely in one hand and turn the paper into the scissors with the other one. By cutting from underneath the paper edges will automatically turn downwards and therefore give a good surface for the glue that you will be applying at the next stage.

When cutting out a complete flower with its stem and leaves, for example, you must leave small pieces of paper between the separate parts of the image to give the cut-out some stability while you are working on it. As you work, cut off and throw away the surplus paper otherwise it can become heavy and get in your way. Cut with the mid-section of the scissor blades unless you are turning a corner, when you can use the point of the scissors to get a sharp outline.

Cutting out with a scalpel

Cutting out with a scalpel knife follows much the same principle as the one using cuticle scissors. You must ensure the scalpel blade is very sharp, otherwise it will tear the paper and, in doing so, could cut your finger or hand. First cut off the surplus paper with ordinary scissors, then place the trimmed image on the self-healing cutting board and place the scalpel blade on an outline. With your other hand, guide the paper towards the blade so it cuts into the paper.

Push the point of the scissors into the paper from above.

Leave bridges of paper between the parts of a large image.

Start cutting out from underneath the picture.

GLUEING

You will need
Mouldable re-usable adhesive or aerosol adhesive
PVA adhesive (white craft glue) or wallpaper paste
Brushes
Sponges
Soft cloths
Tissues or paper towels
Bowl for clean water
Small rubber roller
Small brush or cocktail stick (wooden toothpick)

Glueing your cut-outs on to the object to be découpaged is a very important stage and not one to be hurried over, because any mistakes or short cuts will be glaringly obvious even when the article is finished.

Positioning the cut-outs

After cutting out the images and sealing them if necessary, the next step is to place them on the object you are decorating and move them around until you achieve the desired effect. You'll find that

Or cut out the image with a sharp scalpel knife.

sometimes this is quite a quick process, whereas at other times you can shuffle them around for ages before you're happy with the way they look. Each and every piece of découpage must have a central motif to which the eye is drawn by the overall design. You can do this by linking the design together in various ways which will, of course, be dictated by the central motif. Remember that the space between the cut-outs is just as important as the cut-outs themselves.

If you're decorating a tray, table top or something similar you won't need to hold the cut-outs in place, but when positioning them for a vertical surface, such as the sides of a pot or a chair back, you can either hold the cut-outs in place with small blobs of mouldable re-usable adhesive or by spraying a small amount of aerosol adhesive on the backs – either method is ideal because it allows you to reposition your cut-outs as many times as necessary until you are completely satisfied with them.

Glueing on the cut-outs

In the meantime, pour some of the PVA adhesive (white craft glue) into a clean bowl and dilute it with enough water to make a thin cream and leave it for a few minutes. Alternatively, you can mix up a thin solution of wallpaper paste. When you are absolutely happy with the placings of your cut-outs, carefully remove them from the object and paint the areas you are glueing with the diluted adhesive or paste. Dip your finger in some clean water and rub the glued areas until the surface is as smooth as melted butter. Wash or wipe your hands, then place the cut-outs face down on a clean flat surface and paint their backs with more of the adhesive – this ensures you don't have any glue-free spots underneath the cut-out. Place your first cut-out (usually the one that forms the focal point of the design) on the glue and gently move it around with your fingers until it is in exactly the right place. Make sure your fingers are free from glue when doing this or you might tear the cut-out. Rub gently with either a small clean damp cloth or sponge, or with a rubber roller, from the centre of the cut-out to the outer edges, and press down firmly all around.

Continue with this process until all the cut-outs are stuck down then, using your fingernail, make sure all the edges really are stuck down and that there are no lumps or bumps of glue left in the centre of any cut-out. It is a good idea at this point to dampen a small sponge and gently wipe away any surplus glue from the cut-outs and the article as it is easier to remove at this stage than later on. However, you can leave the glue to dry and then wipe off the surplus if you prefer.

Leave the article to dry for twenty-four hours – it can be tempting to leave it for less but if you varnish the cut-outs before they are completely dry, wet patches will show through the varnish and spoil the finished project.

Move the cut-out around until you are happy with its position.

Paint the back of the cut-out with your chosen adhesive.

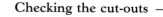

Checking the cut-outs

When the cut-outs are dry, you must wash off all the excess glue if you haven't done so already. Even if you have, it is worthwhile checking that you haven't missed any patches of glue. Check with your fingernail that all the edges of each cut-out are stuck down – the petals of small flowers and corners of leaves, for example, have a nasty habit of lifting. Dip a small paintbrush or cocktail stick (wooden toothpick) into the glue and apply to the recalcitrant pieces. Press down with the sponge, cloth or roller and then wipe away all traces of glue and leave to dry again.

Position the cut-out and smooth down with a sponge.

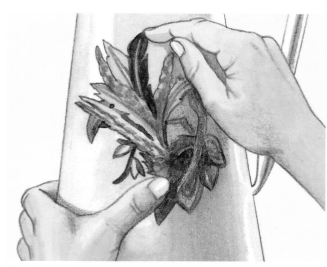

Check that all the edges are stuck down properly.

When the glue is dry, check the edges again.

Wipe away excess glue with a clean damp cloth.

Glue down any unstuck pieces.

Leave to dry then wipe off all traces of glue.

VARNISHING

You will need
2.5–4-cm (1–1½-in) nylon brush
White spirit (paint thinner)
Polyurethane varnish
Tack rag
Wet and dry sandpaper
Finest-grade wire (steel) wool

In the list of materials you need for varnishing we have left out one very important ingredient – patience. If you want to produce the correct effect of découpage, which is to sink the paper cut-outs into the article and make them look as though they have been hand-painted and lacquered, you must apply about twenty coats of varnish to your object. Varnishing is certainly a rather laborious process but one that is essential if you want your découpage to be successful.

Varnish has a very pungent smell, so we recommend working in a well-ventilated room that is as free from dust as possible. Stand the object to be varnished on a clean work surface and protect the floor and your surroundings with sheets of newspaper or dust sheets (drop cloths).

Beginning to varnish

When varnishing it is very important to choose a good-quality brush that won't shed its hairs – a disaster when fine varnishing. Dip the brush into the varnish and drag the tips of the bristles over the edge of the varnish can, then apply the varnish to the article, working from the centre outwards.

Make sure you don't leave a build-up of varnish on the edges, because that will cause drips, and check that you have varnished all the surfaces. When you are satisfied, leave the object to dry for twenty-four hours. Repeat until you have applied between eighteen and twenty coats – the exact number depends upon the thickness of your cut-outs.

You can leave your brush suspended in a jar of white spirit (paint thinner) during this varnishing process, but do make sure it is suspended and not resting on the bristles or you will ruin it.

If you find the varnish is becoming too thick you can thin it down by adding a little white spirit to the can and stirring it well. It is often better to keep your varnish thin because it does tend to thicken up once the can has been opened. It is also a good idea to seal the top of the varnish can with a piece of cling film (plastic wrap) before putting the lid back on to keep some air out.

Apply the paint from the centre outwards.

Leave to dry and seal with varnish if necessary.

Glue on the cut-outs and smooth down.

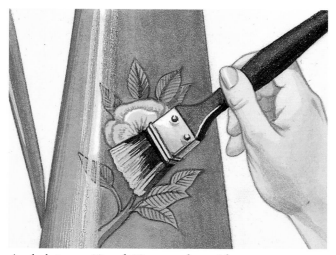

Apply between 18 and 20 coats of varnish.

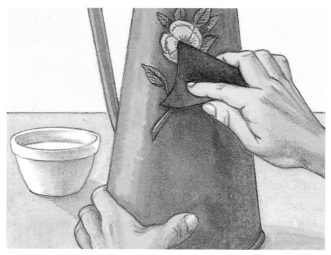

Sand down, wipe clean and apply final coat of varnish.

Sanding down

To achieve a finely lacquered finish, you must now sand down the varnish to give a perfectly smooth surface before applying the final coats of varnish. Soak a sheet of wet and dry sandpaper in a bowl of clean water and sprinkle a lot of water on the varnished surface. Rub fairly hard over the surface (the cut-outs should be submerged under all the varnish and therefore out of harm's way), using a circular motion, until the entire surface has been smoothed out and all particles of dust and other unknown lumps have disappeared. By now you should have a very smooth surface.

If you are unlucky enough to have rubbed away any of the cut-outs now is the time to repair the damage by painting over them. You can use your original background colour but it is a good idea to add a small squeeze of raw umber artists' oil paint to this because the colour will have altered slightly as the coats of varnish built up.

Leave any touching-up to dry, then wipe over the surface with a tack rag. To make this, dip a clean old handkerchief or piece of linen sheeting into some clean water and squeeze dry. Sprinkle with white spirit (paint thinner) and about three teaspoonfuls of varnish, work this mixture into the cloth and then rub it over the surface of the object to remove all traces of dust particles. Leave to dry and apply two coats of satin varnish, letting the first one dry before you apply the second. When the second one has dried, sand it down again with wet and dry sandpaper, then apply another two coats of satin varnish, again letting the first one dry before applying the second.

When the second one has completely dried, sand it down with the very finest wet and dry sandpaper you can find, or use some very fine wire (steel) wool (as used by cabinet makers). When the surface is uniformly dull, stop rubbing and wipe off any particles of dust or wire wool with kitchen paper. Wipe over with a clean damp sponge and leave for about two days before beginning the polishing.

Polishing

You can use any good-quality brand of wax polish for this. Dip a small damp cloth in the polish and begin to rub it over the article. Don't overdo the wax as you can always rub on more as you go. When the surface begins to shine through the wetness, you can buff it hard with a soft dry cloth.

Continue doing this on a daily basis, because the more you polish the article the more shiny and the more durable it will become, safe from marks left by wet glasses and hot dishes.

Rub down with wire (steel) wool or sandpaper.

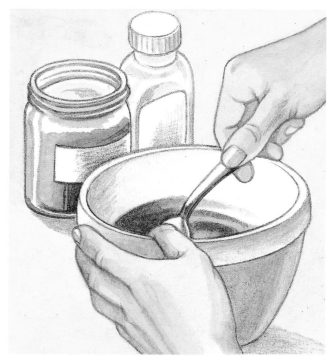

Make a paste of rottenstone powder and baby oil.

Rub it into the surface with a soft damp cloth.

Buff hard with a soft dry cloth. Repeat daily.

ANTIQUING AND AGEING
——— TECHNIQUES ———

There are many objects in this book that have been antiqued to make them look their true age. When working on antique articles, the procedure is different from the fine lacquering technique described on pages 100-2, in which the emphasis is on varnishing and sanding to create a faultless finish. When antiquing, you are trying to create a rougher finish, in which all the cracks and irregular lines that would have come with age are clearly visible.

When you are about to start work on an antique piece, study its age and relevant history and ensure you choose cut-outs that suit its character. One of the most important points with all kinds of découpage is to ensure you are working in a good light and preferably daylight. If that is not possible and you have to work under artificial light, choose a daylight bulb that will not alter the colours of the piece you are working on.

You will need
White spirit (paint thinner)
Rust preventer
Wire brush
Base paint – oil or emulsion (latex)
Selection of paint brushes (all sizes)
Wire (steel) wool (fine to rough grades)
Sandpapers
Powder pigments
Acrylic artists' paints
Artists' oil paints
Old electric or hand egg beater
Polyurethane varnish in matt (flat), silk or gloss
Antique glaze
Sponges
Paper towels
Dust sheets (drop cloths)
PVA (white craft) glue or wallpaper paste
Gum water
Craqueleur
Hair-drier

If you are working on a metal object you must ensure there is no rust, and if you are working on a wooden object you must check it for woodworm. Instructions for removing rust, paint, woodworm and polish are given on pages 93-5. When you have painted your metal object with an anti-rust/undercoat or treated any woodworm in a wooden object, you are ready to apply your emulsion (latex) undercoat.

Applying the undercoat

Do this at random, criss-crossing the brush strokes, and allow to dry for at least twelve hours. Apply

another coat, again criss-crossing the strokes, and leave to dry, then apply the third coat. By now you will see that your base is getting a nicely old and rough look – this is called cross-hatching and gives a linen-like effect. Leave to dry thoroughly.

Apply the gum water and then the emulsion.

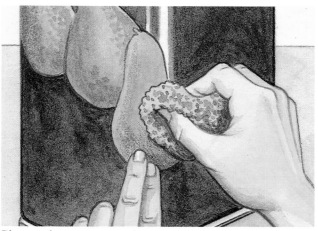

Glue on the cut-outs one by one and smooth down to remove all the air bubbles.

Leave to dry then apply the two coats of craqueleur.

Encourage the cracks to form with a hair-drier. Leave to dry thoroughly.

Apply the coloured oil glaze with a brush or cloth and rub into the cracks and crevices.

Rub off some oil glaze, leaving it in the cracks.

Applying the base coat

Apply the base colour which you have chosen to blend in with the age of the article. To achieve the exact colour, mix a suitably coloured emulsion (latex) paint with the powder pigments or acrylic paints using an egg whisk, or mix an oil-based paint with artists' oil paints, glaze and a little white spirit on a palette.

If you have used emulsion and want a crackled look now is the time to apply a liberal coat of gum water (which can only be used between two coats of emulsion). Allow it to dry, then dip your brush into your emulsion base colour and very carefully go over the entire object, taking great care not to overlap your strokes as that will draw the paint off. As this coat dries, cracks will appear in it. When it is thoroughly dry you are ready to apply an antique glaze to emphasize the cracks.

Applying the antique glaze

This is most effective when working with oil-based paints. To make up your own glaze, mix together the following ingredients:

1 part raw linseed oil
1 part polyurethane varnish
1 part white spirit (paint stripper – not turpentine)

Squeeze a small amount of raw umber, terra verde and perhaps a little black artists' oil paints on to a palette and mix with a little glaze (but keep it thick rather than thin). Rub into the cracks and wipe off the excess. The drying time varies between twelve and twenty hours, depending on the weather conditions. When the glaze has dried completely, apply the first coat of matt varnish and leave to dry.

Placing the cut-outs

Now comes the exciting part of placing your cut-outs on the object you are decorating. To do this, follow the procedures we have described on pages 97-100 and leave to dry for at least twenty-four hours.

Applying the craqueleur

Apply a coat of polyurethane matt (flat) varnish and leave to dry for twenty-four hours. You are now ready to apply the craqueleur, which can be bought in good art supply shops. It can be used over any background and comes in two bottles, one of which contains an oil-based varnish and the other a water-based varnish. Paint on the oil-based varnish and leave to dry until it is still tacky but dry to the touch. Now paint on the water-based varnish – the oil and water act as a catalyst to each other and result in the crackled effect. Don't worry if the craqueleur doesn't work properly the first time, because you can always wipe off this coat with a damp cloth and start again. The cracks are very fine and the process can be accelerated by drying it with a hair-drier. Never attempt to apply a craqueleur to carved surfaces because it can form pools and does not dry properly.

Applying the coloured oil glaze

You are now ready to apply a coloured oil glaze, which is just the same as the antique glaze you have already made with artists' oil paints. To test the colour, if you have had to mix up some more, wipe some of the glaze on to an old piece of board and add more oil paint if necessary. When you are happy with it, rub this coloured glaze on to the object using a brush, piece of soft cloth or even your fingers. Rub off with a soft cloth, taking care to leave the glaze in the cracks and in any areas that would naturally have received a lot of wear and therefore be dirtier, such as the handles and corners. Leave to dry for a couple of days.

Applying fly spots

If you wish to exaggerate the antiquity of the piece you can apply fly spots at this stage, when the coloured oil glaze has dried. Dip a stencilling brush into a bottle of water-based ink, dab off the excess on to a piece of paper or cloth and then spatter it on to the object by rubbing your finger over the bristles. Don't overdo the fly spots! Leave to dry for a minute or two, then dab with an absorbent cloth or paper towel to soften the spots.

Varnishing

When you have finished the antiquing you are ready to start varnishing. You do not want the highly lacquered finish described on pages 100-2 but rather a soft sheen, so apply about twenty coats of matt (flat) polyurethane varnish, then buff with a good-quality wax polish.

Scumble glaze (glaze coat or glazing liquid)

If you don't wish to make your own antique glaze you can use a ready-made scumble glaze (glaze coat or glazing liquid) instead. When using scumble, always thin it down with two parts white spirit (paint thinner) to one part glaze. Experiment with this as the scumble can vary in thickness – the thinner the glaze the faster it will dry.

PITFALLS AND REPAIRS

As with any craft, sometimes you will make mistakes or discover problems when working with découpage. The best way to prevent such mistakes occurring is to be as careful and unhurried over each découpage process as possible but, even then, things will sometimes go wrong. Here is a list of the most common problems we know of and ways to solve them.

Most découpage problems can be solved with the right equipment.

Air bubbles

Sometimes, before you begin to varnish, you will discover air bubbles trapped underneath your cutouts. To remove them, carefully follow a distinct line in the pattern of the cut-out nearest the air bubble, using a sharp scalpel blade. Carefully lift the paper gently and apply a small amount of glue to the underside of the cut-out with a fine paint-brush or a cocktail stick (wooden toothpick). Press the cut-out down firmly, pushing out any excess glue, and wipe away the glue with a damp sponge. Wait until the cut-out is thoroughly dry before beginning the antiquing or varnishing process.

Bloom

If you are varnishing in extreme temperatures, a coat of varnish can dry with a bloom on it. There is only one cure for this – to sand off that coat of varnish and start again.

Craqueleur problems

If you find that your craqueleur has not crackled you can re-apply it by removing the faulty coat and starting again. Wipe off the coat of craqueleur with a sponge or cloth dipped in clean water and wrung out until damp, then re-apply a coat of the oil-based varnish, leave it until it is slightly tacky to the touch and apply a fresh coat of craqueleur.

Damage

If by any chance or through sheer bad luck you drop or knock your finished article and chip a piece off it, you can rectify the problem by taking a fine paintbrush and filling in the hole or crack with varnish. It will take several coats to build up the hole, so leave each one to dry as you would do normally, until the varnish covering the hole stands slightly proud of the rest of the piece. When it is thoroughly dry, sand it back first using fine wet and dry paper and then fine wire (steel) wool.

Rust

If patches of rust should appear on a découpaged object it is because you did not remove all the original rust and prime the object with an anti-rust paint. Sadly, the only remedy is to sand down through all the layers to the original base and the offending patch of rust, apply a small amount of rust remover, followed by some anti-rust paint, and then work back through each stage of the découpage process. We find that this is the sort of mistake you only make once, because it is so heart-breaking that you soon learn the wisdom of taking all those anti-rust measures.

Sanding

If you aren't patient enough when applying your varnish and skimp on the requisite twenty coats, you may have problems when you sand down your varnish before applying the final coats. You may find you have rubbed away the background paint on the corners or sides of flat objects and, occasionally, you might rub away part of the cut-outs themselves. You can repair the damage to the background or cut-out by carefully painting in the required colours with a fine paintbrush, then leaving the paint to dry and varnishing it. If you always apply the twenty or so coats of varnish you shouldn't have this problem when sanding down.

Wrinkles

After a coat of varnish has dried you may notice it has formed wrinkles. This has happened because you didn't stick to the golden rule of allowing one coat of varnish to dry for twenty-four hours before applying the next one. Leave the varnish to dry thoroughly and then, using wet and dry paper, carefully sand away the varnish until all the wrinkles have disappeared.

CARE OF YOUR BRUSHES

It is always a false economy to buy poor-quality brushes because they will shed hairs (irritating at any time but a particular disaster when varnishing) and quickly disintegrate. Buy the best brushes you can afford and be prepared to look after them properly.

Store all your brushes separately, according to their purpose. Each one has a specific job to do – you cannot use an emulsion (latex) brush for one intended for oil paints, or vice versa – so you may find it useful to label the handle of each brush.

We have also given instructions for cleaning sponges and other equipment.

Palettes and paint trays

It is essential to clean these pieces of equipment after use. Wipe off any excess paint with rags, then wash in clean water for emulsion paints and white spirit for oil paints. Pour on some washing-up (dish-washing) liquid and wash well with a clean scrubbing or washing-up brush. Rinse until all traces of the paint have gone and leave to dry.

Rags

Clean rags are invaluable when rubbing off antique glazes because you can simply throw them away when you have finished. However, glaze is highly inflammable, so it is important to dry the rags well (preferably in the open air) before discarding them. Never put them into your rubbish bin (trash can) when wet as they will be highly combustible, and don't be tempted to burn them.

Removing emulsion (latex) paints

Always rinse out your brushes as soon as you have finished using an emulsion (latex) paint. Dip the brush into clean water to remove any surplus paint, then pour some washing-up (dish-washing) liquid into the palm of your hand and push the bristles into it, working them around in a circular motion to coat them in the washing-up liquid. Rinse the brush in hot clean water and hang up to dry. In cases of dire need you can always dry your brush with a hair-drier, but don't hold it too near the brush or you could scorch the bristles.

Removing oil-based paints

While you are working on a project you can leave your brush soaking in a jar of white spirit (paint thinner) but the brush should be suspended in the spirit and not resting on the bottom of the container, otherwise the bristles will lose their shape. When you have finished and want to clean your brushes, wash them in white spirit to remove all traces of the paint. Push the brush firmly into the palm of your hand in order to work the white spirit right up to the metal base (the ferrule) of the brush, then wash the brush under hot running water. Pour some washing-up (dish-washing) liquid into the palm of your hand and push the bristles into it, working them around in a circular motion

to coat them in the washing-up liquid. Rinse thoroughly in clean hot water, shake out the excess moisture and hang the brush up to dry so it keeps its shape.

If you have left your brush for too long before cleaning it you may be able to salvage it by dipping it into a paint stripper diluted with water. Don't leave it in the solution for too long or the hairs will start to drop out! Wash the brush very thoroughly in hot water and hang up to dry in the usual way.

Rust-removing brushes

Rust remover can only be cleaned off using a proprietary cleaner specially made for the purpose. Use the cleaner in a well-ventilated room, rinse the brush well and follow the instructions for brushes used with oil paints.

Sponges

If you use sponges for any découpage work they will also need to be cleaned properly. If you have used an oil-based paint, immerse the sponge in white spirit (paint thinner), squeeze out the excess and wash the sponge in warm soapy water. If your sponge has been used for water-based paint, omit the white spirit and just wash it thoroughly in warm soapy water. Allow to dry naturally.

Varnishing brushes

It is very important to keep these brushes scrupulously clean otherwise they will quickly be ruined. To clean them, follow the instructions for brushes used with oil paints.

Suppliers

*A*ll good hardwear and art shops should supply most of your requirements, but here is a list of suppliers we have found to be particularly helpful. If writing to them and you want a reply, please enclose a stamped addressed envelope.

BRITAIN

J W Bollom
13 Theobalds Road
London WC1X 8FN
Paint suppliers

C Brewer
327 Putney Bridge Road
London SW15 2PQ
Paints, varnishes, crackle mediums, brushes

Brodie & Middleton Ltd
68 Drury Lane
London WC2B 55P
Powder pigments, metallic powder paints, brushes

Compton & Co Ltd
30 Bellevue Road
London SW17 9EF

Paints, powders, varnishes, crackle mediums, brushes

Craig & Rose plc
172 Leith Walk
Edinburgh EH6 5EB
Gold leaf, gold size, transparent oil glaze, extra-pale dedfkat varnish.
Nationwide stockists and paint manufacturers

Crown Berger Europe Ltd
PO Box 37
Crown House
Hollins Road

Darwen
Lancashire BB3 0BG
Large range of oil and emulsion
paints

Daler Rowney Ltd
12 Percy Street
London W1A 2BP
Acrylic, gesso, stencil card, powder
paints, metal leaf

Dover Bookshop
18 Earlham Street
London WC2H 9LN
Specialist books on scraps and
borders for découpage

Green and Stone
259 Kings Road
London SW3 5ER
Crackle mediums, brushes, varnishes

Green and Stone
19 West Market Street
Circencester
Gloucestershire GL2 2AE
Specialists in artists' materials

Hawkins & Co
St Margaret Harleston
Norfolk IP20 0PJ
Découpage scraps (mail order)

John T Keep & Sons Ltd
15 Theobalds Road
London WC1N 5EN
Powder colours, stains, crackle
mediums, brushes, oil glazes

Mamelok Press Ltd
Northern Way
Bury St Edmunds IP32 6NJ
Specialist scrap printers

W Habberley Meadows Ltd
5 Saxon Way
Chelmsley Wood
Birmingham B37 5AY
Specialists in artists' materials

E Milner Oxford Ltd
Clanville Road
Cowley
Oxford OX4 2DB
Powder colours, stains, crackle
mediums, specialist brushes,
transparent oil glazes

John Nyland
80 Norwood Street
London SE27
Powder colours, stains, varnishes,
brushes, crackle mediums, all paints

The Paint Services Co Ltd
19 Eccleston Street
London SW1 9IX
Transparent glazes, varnishes,
specialist brushes

Paper and Paints
4 Park Walk
London SW10
Decorating paints, colour matching,
crackle mediums

E Ploton (Sundries) Ltd
273 Archway Road
London N6 5AA
Specialist brushes, acrylic gesso,
varnishes, crackle mediums

Potmolen Paint
27 Woodcock Industrial Estate
Warminster
Wiltshire BA12 9DX
Specialists in paints, gilding
materials, traditional materials

J H Ratcliffe & Co (Paints) Ltd
135A Linaker Street
Southport PR8 5DF
Brushes, transparent oil glazes

Robertson & Co Ltd
1A Hercules Street
London N7 6AT
Inks, bronze powders, artists' oil
paints, varnishes

Simpson Paints Ltd
122-4 Broadley Street
London NW8 8BB
Transparent oil glazes, gold leaf,
brushes

Stuart R Stevenson
68 Clerkenwell Road
London EC1M 5QA
Gilding, artists' materials

AUSTRALIA
SOUTH AUSTRALIA

Paper and Scraps
The Dolls Boutique
Box 198

Hawthorn
Victoria 3122

Gilly Stephenson
Lot 28
Lacey Road
Mundaring WA 6073
New South Wales

Timberturn
2 Shepley Avenue
Panorama SA 5041
Victoria

NEW SOUTH WALES

Art Smart
50 Ethel Street
Seaforth NSW 2092

Easycraft
56 Hotham Parade
Artarmon NSW 2064

Janet's Art Supplies
145 Victoria Avenue
Chatswood NSW 2067

QUEENSLAND

Art and Craft
45 Targo Street
Bundaberg
Queensland 4670

Oxlades Art Store
Wickham Street
Fortitude Valley
Queensland 4006

Queensland Handicrafts
6 Manning Street
South Brisbane
Queensland 4101

Nerida Singleton
4 Dante Drive
Seven Hills
Queensland 4170

UNITED STATES
*T*he following suppliers are all
registered with the National
Guild of Découpeurs. If you have
any enquiries please contact the
supplier direct.

Cooper's Studio
844 Salem Street

No Andover, MA 01845
Wood boxes, black and white and coloured prints, gold braid and mother of pearl

Découpage Workshop – Carol Perry
858 Woodmont Road
Annapolis, MD 21401
Black and white Japanese woodblock prints. Catalogue available. Authentic faux finishes, unusual gilding techniques and interesting colouring techniques for Japanese woodblock prints. Specific requests welcome

Dew Enterprises – Don Woodegeard
6232 Hickory Creek Road
High Point, NC 27263
Furniture, plant stands, drop leaf coffee and end tables, many more unfinished products, custom plaques, furniture or tole painting brochures

Harrower House
Rd No 1, Box 196
Blairstown, NJ 17825
Wooden boxes, découpage mucilage, Victorian gold paper trim, black and white pillement prints, coloured prints – French eighteenth-century

Houston Art & Frame Inc
Box 56146
Houston, TX 77227
Assortment of découpage supplies, write for information

Illinois Bronze Paint Company
300 East Main Street
Lake Zurich, IL 50047
Write for catalogue

Kurfees Coatings Inc
201 East Market Street
Louisville, KY 40202
Latex finish, 288 Aqua-Lite Acrylic Latex Sealer and Finish, Satin Clear

Lee Walker's Designs Galore
0962 Sun King
Glenwood Springs, CO 81601
Colour and black and white prints especially for découpage with non-fading inks. Catalogue and prints

Les Boiseries – Jacqueline Correa
1001 Spiritridge
Cincinnati, OH 45252
Prints in black and white for lamps, trays and furniture. Seminars available on all phases of découpage in studio or out of town. Catalogue of prints, lamps and pencils available

McCloskey Varnish Co
7600 State Road
Philadelphia, PA 19136
Polyurethane finish: Heirloom Crystal Clear Polyurethane and Heirloom Crystal Clear Acrylic Varnish (non-yellowing with age)

Allan R Mitchell
10347 Somerset
Detroit, MI 48224
Wood boxes; prints, black and white and coloured. Instruction manuals. Ship anywhere. Write for specific request

Fred Pagel
1535 Aline Drive
Grosse Pointe Woods, MI 48236
Black and white prints

Plaid Enterprises Inc
PO Box 7600
Norcross, GA 30091-7600
Finishes, thinner, découpage paste, gloss and matt acrylic sprays, aerosol sealer, paints, stains, antiquings, decal mediums, wax, glue, gesso, gold leaf sizing. Write for catalogue

Priscilla's Publications and Products
8158 East 44th Street
PO Box 45730
Tulsa, OK 74145
Painting supplies and finishes. Write for catalogue

Singerie – Phillip David Robb
2052 High Tower Drive
Hollywood, CA 90068
Catalogue available, black and white prints

Walnut Hollow
Dodgeville, WI
Wood boxes and other wood products. Mail order service. Toll-free call: 1-800-243-2089 for catalogue and ordering

Wildlife Lithographs Inc
510 East Fellows Street
Dixon, IL 61021
Large selection wildlife prints. Write for catalogue. Clocks and accessories

National Guild of Découpeurs
807 Rivard Boulevard
Grosse Pointe, MI 48230

INDEX

ACKNOWLEDGEMENTS

Debbie Patterson would like to thank the following for their kind help in loaning props:

Chenil Galleries
181 Kings Road
London SW3

556 Antiques
556 Kings Road
London SW6

Gallery of Antique Costume and Textiles
2 Church Street
London NW8

Global Village
247 Fulham Road
London SW3

Ann May
80 Wandsworth Bridge Road
London SW6

Magpie
152 Wandsworth Bridge Road
London SW6

Perfect Glass
5 Park Walk
London SW10

Risky Business
44 Church Street
London NW8

The publishers would like to thank the following people for their kind help in loaning historic articles for photography:

Michel André Morin (Antiques),
12b Camden Passage
on Charlton Place,
London N1

Dermot and Jill Palmer (Antiques),
7-8 Union Street,
The Lanes, Brighton,
East Sussex.

Many of the objects in this book were bought at boot fairs, which we realize are purely British events. The nearest American or Australian equivalents would be yard sales or flea markets.

If you wish to follow the instructions for antiquing your découpage pieces, you can buy various proprietary brands of crackle medium, or use gum arabic, which is what we have suggested in this book. However, gum arabic can only be used on a background of emulsion (latex), not oil-based paint It is an excellent crackle medium and can either be bought ready diluted as gum water or as gum arabic crystals, which are dissolved in boiling water – use 450g (1lb) crystals to 1-2 litres (2-3 pints) water. Add a drop of washing-up (dish-washing) liquid and use as instructed on page 104.

— A Warning About — Copyright and Copying

If you want to use an existing design, such as one taken from a sheet of wrapping paper, or copy a design from a book or magazine, you should first check whether or not the design is in copyright. This also applies if you plan to have the design photocopied or scaled up or down. Most publishers are normally happy to give such permission, provided that your design is not for commercial use.